BUILDING STRONGER FAMILIES

Royce Money

While this book is designed for your personal
enjoyment, it is also intended for group study. A
Leader's Guide with Victor Multiuse Transparen-
cy Masters is available from your local bookstore
or from the publisher.

VICTOR

BOOKS a division of SP Publications, Inc.
WHEATON, ILLINOIS 60187

Offices also in
Whitby, Ontario, Canada
Amersham-on-the-Hill, Bucks, England

Recommended Dewey Decimal Classification: 301.42
    Suggested Subject Heading: FAMILY

Library of Congress Catalog Card Number: 83-51300
ISBN: 0-88207-244-7

VICTOR BOOKS
A division of SP Publications, Inc.
        Wheaton, Illinois 60187

Contents

Foreword

*W*e are indebted to Royce Money for the excellent and unique book he has put together on building stronger families. The book is filled with great insight and wisdom. The author has provided the reader with information that is well-founded by research and presented with illustrated, how-to guidelines for building family strengths.

The book is action-oriented, practical, and a delight to read. It is filled with interesting examples which make it easy for readers to apply the principles to their own lives.

Building Stronger Families can greatly benefit a wide variety of people. It is for:

- anyone who lives in a family
- anyone who is married or considering marriage
- persons having family problems
- those who want to make a good family life better
- spouses who want a better relationship
- parents who want a better relationship with their children
- anyone who is interested in developing more positive interpersonal relationships.

The book will also be of great interest to leaders of churches that currently have a family ministry program or are considering starting such a program.

Royce Money offers a workable plan for home, church, and community to build stronger families. His book deserves to be read by families everywhere.

Dr. Nick Stinnett, Chairman and Professor
Department of Human Development and the Family
The University of Nebraska—Lincoln

To the dear Christians
of South National Church of Christ
Springfield, Missouri
who helped turn a dream of family ministry
into a reality

Section 1

1
How Do You Build a Strong Family?

*G*ood question, isn't it. It's not easy living together as a family. A lot of them aren't making it very well. Yet, I noticed recently that surveys of groups as diverse as graduating seniors, *Fortune 500* chief executive officers, and subscribers to *Playboy* magazine all want the same thing more than anything else—strong family relationships. God created us to grow up in families and, for most of us, to form families of our own. But in that God-ordained pattern of life lies a multitude of frustrations, disappointments, and heartaches. Why does it have to be this way? Or does it?

I don't believe that it does. As I look around I see a lot of families who are making it. They are loving one another and growing together and liking it. To be sure, they have their problems, but life for them is more than struggling from one crisis to another. As a marriage and family counselor and family minister, I see many things that are wrong with our families. Those gloomy statistics of divorce, unfaithfulness, child abuse, and family violence are all too familiar. This book is about something else, though. It is a practical, down-to-earth look at how families and the people in them can grow stronger in their relationships.

We have all heard the glowing discourses on "God's Plan for the Family" that leave us feeling frustrated and inadequate. The picture of the "ideal" Christian family is so far from where I live that there is little similarity. This "heavenly" picture of the home is so unrealistic that it produces either guilt or indifference on the part of those who don't measure up.

My promise to you as a fellow struggler working to build a strong family is that I will be realistic and honest and human. Families have to *learn* to deal with pain, frustration, disappointment, and conflict, as well as with the joys that come from living together. Within the marvelous entity we call a family lies the potential for the most rewarding human experiences known to man or for a literal hell on earth. In our time together we're going to aim for the former, but do so in a realistic and practical way.

A Question of Priorities

A few years ago, I was speaking to a civic club in Springfield, Missouri. It was the week before Thanksgiving, so I thought about doing something to connect the season with my favorite theme—strengthening families. After the normal amount of levity that is characteristic of the beginning of these speeches (and their usual jabs at my last name), I passed out index cards. My request was for them to list on the card five things that they valued highly. These could be a person, a task, a concept—anything they saw as dear to them. In a surprisingly short time they were finished. Then I delivered the bad news. One of the items had to be eliminated. With great groaning and carrying on, each one marked through an item on his list. Then came more bad news. Another item had to be eliminated, and then still another. Not so much groaning now. This was becoming serious. They were left with two items on the card.

I assured them that I would not be so cruel as to force yet

another choice. But I was curious as to what two items remained on these cards. "How many have something about family left on your cards?" Almost every hand went up. "How many have something about your religion or your relationship to God?" Almost every hand went up again.

The jobs, the hobbies, the political freedoms many of them cherished, all took a back seat to family and God in this game of forced choices they were asked to play. I then asked a final question. "How is the way you spend your time reflecting those ultimate priorities?" This time no grumbling, no rattling of water glasses, just silence.

This book is about those two priorities. I've noticed in my own life and in observing other people how tragedy immediately causes us to prioritize our lives in an amazingly accurate fashion. Suddenly our thoughts and actions are riveted on the people involved and on the spiritual realm that becomes so real and necessary for Christians at such times. The trivial and the optional and the fringe concerns are quickly swept aside in favor of the ultimate issues that need our attention.

Do you think perhaps we could do some of that on a regular basis and not have to wait for the tragedies in life to teach us lessons? I believe we can. And one way to do it is to focus our attention on increasing the quality of our family relationships and our relationship with God. They do go together beautifully.

For the Christian, attention to one dimension will reap its benefits in both. Stronger families will produce stronger churches. Therefore, growing stronger families should be a top priority in every church. After all, if Christianity doesn't work in the home, where on earth can we expect it to work? The Christian family is the laboratory for Christian living. Growing strong families is not optional; it is essential if the church is to have a meaningful message to a dying world.

In Search of Strong Families

In the mid-1970s, Dr. Nick Stinnett, then professor of family studies at Oklahoma State University, became interested in learning more about what makes for strong families. As he studied family conditions in our nation, he was disturbed that much of the research and popular literature about families focused on what was wrong with them. While recognizing the validity of such an emphasis, he, nevertheless, saw a crying need for balance. More information was needed about positive family models and what strong families are like. Knowing that most of us learn much more effectively when we see how something *should* be done, rather than how it *shouldn't*, he set out to fill the void of information available on family strengths.

He began to study strong families in Oklahoma and shortly thereafter expanded his research to the entire nation and beyond. For families to qualify, they had to demonstrate a high degree of marital happiness, a high degree of parent-child satisfaction, and appear to meet each other's needs to a high degree.

Through questionnaires and interviews, many families were investigated. Their patterns of relationship, communication, conflict, and power structure were closely evaluated. When the information was processed, six qualities surfaced in a remarkably high percentage of these families.
- Appreciation expressed
- Good communication patterns
- Time spent together
- Commitment to family
- High degree of religious orientation
- Ability to deal with crisis in a positive manner.

The beautiful thing about Stinnett's findings is that these qualities apply equally in strengthening single parent families and step-families. The fact that this research was with families where both parents were present in the home, having been married only to each other, does not diminish one bit the positive impact of these characteristics on other family forms. In fact, I believe that they would be *especially* effective in dealing with the complexities and feelings of loss in families who have had to deal with death or divorce.

To broaden the horizons even farther, the qualities we are going to examine will strengthen any interpersonal relationship. I am continually amazed at how much God's Word has to say about how to get along with one another. I am confident that you could open the New Testament at random and find on any page something to do with how we are to get along with one another.

In 1 John 4, the beloved Apostle John reminds us that we can't say we love God and yet fail to get along with one another. Jesus reminds us in His model prayer and the comments following that if we do not forgive our fellowmen, God will not forgive us (Matt. 6:12 ff). Is it too much of an exaggeration to say that God will deal with us in the same manner that we treat one another? I think not. James makes the point in rather straightforward fashion when he reminds us that "judgment without mercy will be shown to anyone who has not been merciful" (James 2:13). Sounds to me like we would all profit greatly by learning how to build stronger human relationships wherever we find them.

A Personal Word
Before I discuss these six qualities, I want to say a personal word about Dr. Stinnett. He is now chairman of the Department of Human Development and the Family at the University of Nebraska in Lincoln. He is a mentor of mine and a close personal friend. Of more importance, he is a committed Christian man who, along with his associates, is making a tremendous contribution to this nation's family life in emphasizing family strengths.

As Nick and I were talking about his findings, we were

both struck by the fact that his six qualities of strong families have an abundance of support through the Scriptures. That is no surprise to us who are Christians. But it needs to be said to a lot of other people that the principles of Christianity when applied in the family context will produce strong families. And we Christians need to be reminded specifically how it can be done.

I don't have much trouble seeing how the various admonitions of Jesus or Paul or other biblical authorities are to affect my relationships with Christian brothers and sisters or even people who are not Christians. My difficulty comes in seeing how they apply to the way I am to treat members of my own family, and especially my children. Where does it say in Scripture that parents have the right to be disrespectful to their children, simply because they are older and are in charge? Where does it say that biblical principles of interpersonal relationships apply only on an adult-to-adult basis? Well, it doesn't say that; yet we sometimes act as if it does. What a shame that we Christians are all too often more courteous to strangers than we are to members of our own families.

With Nick Stinnett's permission, and his gracious encouragement, I want to share with you these six qualities of strong families, adding to his work my own observations and the Scripture references that so beautifully reinforce his findings. Section 1 is designed to give practical suggestions on how a Christian family can grow closer to each other and to God.

Section 2 is really an expansion of the first part to include the family of God—the church. Its purpose is to show how a congregation of any size can develop family ministries that will strengthen its families. In a practical, step-by-step fashion, we will explore ways that collective efforts to build better marriages and families can be accomplished.

The task of building strong families is not optional to the

church but lies at the heart of Christianity. The quality of the church's existence and well-being depends on whether it can continue to produce godly families who love one another and mirror in that relationship God's love. It is to that task that we now turn our attention.

2
Expressing Appreciation

O ne of the most significant qualities Dr. Stinnett discovered was that strong families consistently express appreciation for each other. They build one another up psychologically and make others feel good about themselves. This practice was found to be pervasive throughout the families studied.

Isn't it interesting how we gravitate toward those who make us feel good? Every Sunday at church I make it a point to seek out certain people who will have a good word of encouragement. I do the same at the university where I teach and in social settings. I've got to have a pretty consistent dose of that. I thrive on it. How about you?

To be sure, there are times when I need to deal with negative matters. But I can't take a steady diet of criticism and negativism and not be adversely affected by it.

It's a great human need—the need to be appreciated. And we shouldn't be surprised to learn that this need is intensified when it is placed in the context of those who matter most to us—our very own family. When total strangers or casual acquaintances fail to show appreciation or build us up, we may take passing note of the fact, but it will hardly ruin our day. But when we fail to get any type of positive response from our very own—what a blow!

In my own family, Pam and I have made a concentrated effort to set a tone of positive reinforcement in our relationship with each other and our two daughters. It hasn't been easy and we occasionally lapse into negative patterns. But when we do practice the positive patterns, the results in the quality of our family relationships are amazing.

The negative effects of a critical spirit on a family were brought home to me in a graphic way that I will never forget. It happened a few years ago on a Wednesday night. As is our custom, we were at our midweek Bible study at the church. The day had not gone well for me for some reason that I can't even recall. After the classes were over, I was really anxious to get home. As we began to leave, the girls were nowhere in sight. A quick tour of the building produced nothing but more frustration. I finally found them playing with some of their friends. Instead of thanking God that they enjoyed coming to church and being with Christian friends, I angrily told them to get in the car.

As we left the church parking lot, I began my critical lecture, tearing down their sweet spirits because they had inconvenienced me a bit. It seemed that I had done nothing but criticize in my communication with them the entire day. After the initial barrage of woes that would befall them if it ever happened again (you know the speech), Jennifer, who was about eight at the time, just couldn't take it any longer. "Gripe! Gripe! Gripe!" she blurted out in exasperation. "That's all I've heard all day. Doesn't anybody have anything good to say?"

By that time we were approaching a traffic light that was red. Her statement hit me like the proverbial ton of bricks. She was right! As we waited for that light to change, we all made a promise to each other that in what was left of that day, we would only say good things to and about each other.

That night as we were going to bed, I asked Jennifer to forgive my critical spirit and I asked God to instill in me a spirit of positive affirmation of those I love the most in all this world. That experience was a turning point for me. It helped me to see more clearly than ever that my wife and children need from me a continual flow of expressed appreciation, just as I need it from them.

Compliments and Criticisms

Communications experts say that verbal content in the home should be at least 80 percent positive.[1] The negative cannot and should not be completely eliminated. However, the negative produces maximum results only within a context of frequently expressed positive affirmation. Encouragement builds self-respect and a sense of accomplishment.

I notice with fascination the Apostle Paul's customary pattern of correcting and admonishing the recipients of his letters. He would often begin with a series of compliments about how well they were doing in certain aspects of their faith. Then he would deal with the problems at hand, often in rather direct fashion. Finally, he would close the letter with further encouragement and affirmation. With the exception of his letter to the Galatians (in which he was really upset), Paul followed this pattern.

I call it the sandwich method of dealing with a problem. The negative issue is sandwiched or cushioned between two positive affirmations. Perhaps in imitating Paul's method as we encounter both children and adults, we will leave the delicate self-image of the person more intact. And this method will help us distinguish between affirming the person and *not* affirming a particular aspect of his behavior.

I don't know what it is about a criticism, but somehow it outweighs a compliment. If I had some scales that could measure emotional impact, I am confident that the negatives would far outweigh the positives. When I speak to various groups about families, I am always interested (and probably a bit sensitive) about people's reactions to what I said. On one occasion after a speech, about fifteen people stopped by to tell me how much they appreciated my remarks. One fellow, however, wasn't all that impressed, and proceeded to tell me how I could have improved it. That night when I got home, Pam asked, "How did it go?" "They didn't like it," was my hasty reply. I had remembered the one criticism and forgotten the fifteen compliments. Fortunately, my wife has learned to say, "Tell me about it," when she suspects that she doesn't have the whole truth. After I recounted the rest of the story, she helped me get the experience back into better perspective. But those negative comments surely do take their toll, don't they?

In my counseling through the years, it grieves me to think of the number of people who have said to me, "I never could please my mother or daddy," or "My parents never complimented me on anything. They only pointed out my faults." The damage done by these unthinking and insensitive parents is extremely hard to overcome in adulthood, and some people never quite do.

I have noticed something else in my marriage counseling. I don't ever recall seeing a couple whose marriage was failing where there was not an absence of mutual positive reinforcement. Every troubled couple had ceased to see the good and the beautiful in their partners. But rest assured that each was an expert on what was wrong with the other!

I recall on one occasion I was trying to referee a quarreling match between a husband and wife. Seeing that the hurling of insults and criticisms was getting us nowhere, I said to the husband, "Tell me what you like about your wife." The request startled him so much that he could not answer for quite awhile. His mind had been in a faultfinding track for so long that my question seemed utterly foreign to him.

On another occasion I had a couple tell what each appreciated about the other. I then asked, "How long has it been since you have heard words like these?" They both said, "A long time." "How does it feel?" I inquired. "It feels really good," they said in unison. That experience was a turning point in their marriage. They realized what millions of people are failing to realize—that *appreciation needs to be expressed often for a relationship to grow.*

Somehow we men get the notion that expressing deep feelings is not the manly thing to do. Nothing could be further from the truth. We are letting our secular culture determine a view of masculinity that is not in accord with the Bible or good mental health. Feelings of gratitude need to be expressed while there can still be a blessing for the giver as well as for the receiver.

Perhaps I should add that appreciation should be expressed just for "being" as well as for "doing." It is easier to express thanks to a person who has done something for you. But in some circumstances the appreciation needs to be given aside from any services or favors that are performed. We are such a performance-oriented society that we easily slip into the mind-set of connecting our appreciation in cause-and-effect fashion to a deed. Yet, as I think of my children and my wife, I love and appreciate them simply for what they are and what they mean to me. I don't want them to ever think that they are esteemed only for what they are able to do for me. On those days when everything seems to go wrong, I take great comfort in knowing that there are those who love me, no matter what. They love *me*, and not just my activity.

The Bible and Building Up
Does the Bible have much to say about people expressing appreciation to one another and building up and encouraging one another? It certainly does. Remember, these Scrip-

ture admonitions apply to family relationships as well as to our dealings with people in general. The first one that comes to mind is a favorite of mine, found in Ephesians 4:29. "Do not let any unwholesome talk come out of your mouths, but only what is helpful for building others up according to their needs." What a powerful verse! Here is one of those passages that—if it were applied in earnest by every member of a family—would revolutionize that family. What if your family decided today to say only what built others up and to respond to one another on the level of what was really needed? Would the future be any different from the past? Nearly all of us would have to say, "Yes, it most certainly would."

The Thessalonian correspondence is full of encouragement from Paul. On several occasions Paul encouraged and admonished them to encourage one another. That spirit was exemplified by his comment in 1 Thessalonians 5:11: "Therefore encourage one another and build each other up, just as in fact you are doing."

How we need that! We need it in the home and in the church. As we Christians live in the precarious position of being *in* the world but not *of* the world, we meet discouragement and frustration at every turn. Surely we can make the atmosphere of our biological families and our spiritual families different from the way the world treats us. As I understand it, "build each other up" is the opposite of "tear each other down." God help us to see the difference.

I think also of the Samaritan leper in Luke 17 who was healed and returned to thank Jesus—the only one in a group of ten who had a new lease on life. I think of the countless instances in the Bible where appreciation was expressed to God for His infinite blessings. Applying the biblical principles we have already discussed, there is likely to be a direct connection between a person's thankfulness to God and his expressions of appreciation to fellow human beings.

Conversely, the lack of such an expression in one probably will be manifested in the other.

Some Suggestions

What are some practical things your family can do to cultivate the habit of expressing appreciation to each other, thus strengthening your relationships?

• Gather your family together and have each member tell what he or she appreciates about the others. No mixed messages allowed, such as, "I like you, even though you're overweight." Keep it completely positive. Another hint, make the comments specific, such as, "I appreciate Mom because she is patient with me when I have trouble deciding what to wear." It can be appreciation for actions, qualities, attitudes, or just being there. This exercise can be done at the dinner table, on special occasions, during a family time, or even riding in a car during a trip.

• Have each family member make out an "I feel appreciated" list. It goes like this: each person is to list five things that other members of the family can do that make him or her feel appreciated, cared for, and loved. At the top of the page, write "I feel appreciated when . . ." and list the items.

A few guidelines: the items have to be *specific*, *repeatable*, *noncontroversial*, and *inexpensive* or, preferably, free. For example, Dad might write, "I feel appreciated when Johnny empties the trash without having to be reminded." Mom might say, "I feel appreciated when everyone puts his or her dirty clothes in the hamper." Johnny could say, "I feel appreciated when Dad plays catch with me after dinner." Someone might say, "I feel appreciated when Mom cooks my favorite meal." And on and on the list could go.

Appreciation is expressed in many ways. One of the most significant ways is in action. The strength of the "I feel appreciated" exercise is that everyone in the family has an increased awareness of what makes the others feel appreciated. It eliminates guesswork and mindreading. Maybe you would like to put these lists up on the refrigerator door, or wherever your family displays its "important papers."[2]

• Develop the habit of giving each member at least one compliment a day. Charlie Shedd gives his wife a compliment a day, with a completely new one each week. Sound corny? Granted, if you are not in the habit of doing this already, it may be a bit mechanical and awkward at first. But it is a habit that pays tremendous rewards. Commitment to this habit will cause you to look for positive attributes in others. The important thing is to make a decision to do it and not wait until you feel like it. In the spirit of true *agape* love, decide how you are going to act toward your family, regardless of the presence of some negative personal feelings—yours or theirs.

• Make it a point to be aware of your speech patterns in dealing with your family members, to see how much of your communication is positive and how much is negative. Perhaps you can do this on your own; but if you'd like some help—and if you are brave—try asking your family how you are coming across to them most of the time. I hope that your vulnerability will be met with the truth spoken in love. Rarely are we objective enough about our own communication habits to judge ourselves accurately.

I dare say that if some of us had a tape recording of certain portions of our family communication, we would be shocked, embarrassed, and ashamed of the way we sound. Now if you're *really* brave, you can try that little experiment.

• Set a proper tone for your family. Remember that positive breeds positive and negative breeds negative. Whether you like it or not, you must admit that family members key off one another. Your family is a system, and what affects one person has an effect on the others. You can think of times when one cheerful person set a positive tone for the entire family. And you can recall some times when the reverse was true. You can be the tone-setter in your family by deciding to act and react in a positive manner.

The minds God gave us are powerful instruments. Over and over the Lord reminds us that we tend to become what we think about—what we set our minds on doing. In Paul's words to the Ephesians, the assumption is that everyone needs building up (4:29). That is not a point of discussion. What matters is *how* a person can be built up or encouraged—according to what he *needs*.

What does your family need? I can assure you that more encouragement and appreciation expressed in word and deed is on everybody's list. Strong families do that often, but even the best could use a little more. God give us more sons and daughters of encouragement!

Footnotes

1. H. Norman Wright, *The Family That Listens* (Wheaton, Ill.: Victor Books, 1978), p. 84.
2. Adapted from Richard B. Stuart, *Helping Couples Change: A Social Learning Approach to Marital Therapy* (New York: The Guilford Press, 1980), pp. 192-208.

3
Developing Communication Patterns

*O*ne of the basic threads in a strong family is healthy communication patterns. It is basic because to some extent all the other qualities take their strength from the ability of family members to communicate clearly.

Even strong families have squabbles and disagreements. But they are able to work through the issues that divide them and keep them from becoming full-blown problems. So the difference between healthy families and failing families is not the presence or absence of conflict, but the way in which conflict is handled.

Have you ever wondered what enables some families to work through differences successfully, while others seem to disintegrate before your very eyes? I don't pretend to have all the answers to that question, by any means, but I have noticed something through the years. One thing that enables healthy families to work through difficulties is that they have a good track record of successes—of past issues negotiated and settled. Their relationships do not stand or fall on the outcome of any one problem. They have a firm commitment to the family that is aside from the outcome of any one issue.

We need to be reminded again that family members operate as a *system*. Whatever change takes place in one has some effect on all the others. Within that incredibly complex system comes our sense of self—of who we really are. Two elements in particular determine our identity as individuals, a sense of belonging to the family group and a sense of separateness from that same group.[1] How these two forces are mixed determines a large part of who we think we are.

The way that we convey these messages about each other is called *communication*. The process of sending and receiving messages to, from, and about one another in a family is more critical than in outside contacts. We attach more significance to what those we love think of us. It is no surprise, then, that good relationships depend on the transmission of information.

But information comes in all sorts of forms. There is most obviously the content, the actual words. Yet, we can't stop there. Norman Wright reminds us that the actual words of a message comprise only about 7 percent of the total communication. The other 93 percent includes voice tone (38 percent) and all nonverbals (55 percent), not to mention the subjective viewpoints of both the sender and the receiver of a message.[2]

Are you sufficiently confused by now about how we human creatures in clusters called families ever get anything done? It is pretty complicated, but let me simplify it a little by suggesting that we focus in on the *how* of family communication instead of *what*. The key is to examine *patterns* of family communication rather than the actual words that are being said.

Have you ever noticed that in a family conversation, no matter what subject is being discussed, the pattern is pretty much the same? It's rather predictable who's going to object, who is likely to lose patience first, who talks the most, the least, etc. In destructive family communication, it is this pattern that must be altered for true change to occur. This pattern is called the *family process—how* the family talks to each other. Altering the content information is somewhat helpful, but by far the most helpful for change is to alter the process.

The importance and accuracy of process investigation can be illustrated easily. But first, make a note that when the *content* (the words) of your message and the *process* (everything else besides the actual words) contradict, *the process is always believed.* A simple experiment can be done with pets or with infants. They key their response to process levels of communication. You can call a dog or an infant every name in the book (and a few that aren't), and if you smile and have a pleasant voice tone and tender touch, they will respond positively.

Come to think of it, babies and pets aren't the only ones who respond on the process level. We adults do the same. What about the father who says to his kids, "More than anything else, I would like to spend more time with you," but doesn't? What about one spouse who says to another in deadpan monotone, and with no touching, "Honey, I surely do love you!" Is it believed?

Family communication improves when the process level— how the family communicates—is realized, examined, and changed for the better. The rest of the chapter is devoted to a list of characteristics that are found in the communication patterns of healthy families. Notice that the emphasis is not on *what* is said but on *how* it is said—on the pattern and the atmosphere. At the end of the list will be some guidelines for discovering and evaluating your family process.

Speaking the Truth in Love
Paul told the Ephesians that one of the marks of maturing persons is that they "speak the truth in love" (4:15). That exact quality, when exercised by family members toward

one another, will produce the same maturing, healthy effect. Truth and love make a perfect pair. From a Christian perspective, it's hard to picture one without implying the other. John, the apostle of love, in his brief second letter, blended the two concepts beautifully, as he did in his other writings as well.

Speaking the truth in love within a family context implies that people talk directly with one another and do not use devious patterns that tend to hide or twist the truth. There are times when love tends to win out over truth—when we try to protect others in the family from the truth that hurts. And sometimes the truth does hurt, but love demands that we face it. On the other hand, when truth wins out to the neglect of love, this hurtful kind of truth can force alienation between loved ones.

Truth and love, when joined together, can provide a powerful force in the process of family communication. Through inspiration Paul reminded us, "Love does not delight in evil but rejoices with the truth" (1 Cor. 13:6). May they ever be united as we "put off falsehood and speak truthfully" to one another, yet do it "in love" (Eph. 4:25, 15).

Mutual Respect and Consideration

I suppose that's another way of saying that healthy families are unselfish, and their communication mirrors that attitude. We hear a lot in Christian circles today about servant leadership, particularly as it applies to church leaders. But those same qualities, when applied to family relationships, produce marvelous results. A Christian father has no right as a servant leader to order his wife or children to serve his own personal interests and selfish comforts. Surely a part of children's "honoring" of father and mother—the first commandment with a promise—is to show a basic respect and consideration for them (Eph. 6:1-2; Deut. 5:16).

Two passages in the New Testament capture the essence of this quality so very well. Remember that these passages are to be applied to *family* relationships as well as other interpersonal contacts. Let me help you by taking small liberties with the text:

• "(In your family) get rid of all bitterness, rage and anger, brawling and slander, along with every form of malice. Be kind and compassionate to one another, forgiving each other, just as in Christ God forgave you" (Eph. 4:31-32).

• "Therefore, as God's (family), holy and dearly loved, clothe yourselves with compassion, kindness, humility, gentleness and patience. Bear with each other and forgive whatever grievances you may have against one another. Forgive as the Lord forgave you. And over all these virtues put on love, which binds them all together in perfect unity" (Col. 3:12-14).

I believe with all my heart that if any family completely dedicated themselves to living out these two passages, it would revolutionize that family! Would you like to try it?

Free Expression of Feelings

How are feelings handled in your family? Chances are that you deal with feelings somewhat like one or both of your parents did when you were growing up. Feelings are God-given and are an important part of our life. Your children are likely to deal with feelings the way they see you deal with them. That could range from virtual supression of all feelings to being wide open to their expression.

One thing is clear. Strong families encourage the free expression of feelings—both positive and negative. The males are as free to express feelings as the females. There is no relegating of feelings to females only. Toughness for the men is not tied to the stifling of emotions. Norman Wright points out another problem created by cut-off male feelings:

A husband or father who is alienated from his own feelings cannot accept emotional expressions from others. This creates two problems for his family. He denies good emotional acceptance and expression in his own family and he has difficulty in satisfying the needs of his child and spouse for affection. Gentle emotions such as kindness, affection, appreciation, compassion, reverence, concern, wistfulness, and sadness may not only not be demonstrated by the father but unappreciated when shared by others in his household. The alienation of emotions is something we have learned. Getting in touch with our emotions can be learned too.[3]

The emotions we experience are neither right nor wrong. They are natural. That is why we should never say to another person, "You shouldn't feel that way." Granted, there may not be a rational foundation for their feelings, but the feelings are there, nonetheless. Empathetic families have learned to respond to the feeling level of a person rather than issue a judgment on the validity of the feeling.

While feelings are natural, that is not to say that any action stemming from the feeling is permissible. The Bible talks a lot about emotions and feelings, but it in no way condones the indiscriminate acting out of them. Positive change takes place by the "renewing of your mind" (Rom. 12:2) and by what we think about and decide to do (Phil. 4:8-9).

So much could be said about the need for granting permission in a family to deal with emotions. We need for people to say, "It's all right to feel angry, but it isn't all right to act it out in unhealthy and unchristian ways." A family becomes stronger when members are in touch with what is going on inside one another. No guessing. No wondering. Just an empathetic and accepting atmosphere where people who love one another very much can be open and vulnerable and can share in that deepest part of their lives.

Individual Differences Recognized and Accepted

How much pressure is there in your family to conform? To all act and think alike? That's the issue here. Strong families allow for individual differences and even encourage them in some areas. Children differ markedly in temperament. Yet parents may want to raise all their children the same way and want them all to turn out the same.

Children in a family can be pretty different. I know that's true in our family. Alison, our older daughter, was a compliant baby, had an easy disposition, and regular eating and sleeping habits. Her sister who came along two and one-half years later differed from that pattern significantly. It would have been very easy for us to decide that Jennifer varied from the "acceptable" norm. We could have reminded her in subtle ways all her life that being "different" was wrong. Of course, our view of what was "acceptable" and "different" was heavily colored by our experience of rearing Alison. Different is not wrong. It's just different.

Let me brag just a little. Our two daughters have delightful personalities and are a joy to be around. Yet they are very different in temperament and in physical appearance. For that matter, my wife and I are significantly different in temperament. Thank God for "different"! Wouldn't life be a drag without it? I can't think of anything more boring than to be married to someone exactly like me.

Differences in strong families are seen as something special to be valued. For children to grow toward autonomy— that precious individual self—permission must be given to them to be different from others in the family. To be that way is not a threat to unity and family solidarity. It is a mark of strength.

Skillful Negotiation Through Conflicts

My friend and colleague, Dr. Tom Milholland, has done extensive research on problem-solving techniques. They originally were intended for husbands and wives, but with slight adaptation they can fit most family situations. Since the successful resolution of problems and conflicts is essential for growth in relationships, we need to take a close look at these steps.

• Each one should listen carefully and express his or her own feelings. That involves owning up to one's own feelings, expressing them, and listening to the other's feelings with equal interest.

• Explore the problem area. This step involves discussing the present problem and expressing one's own feelings about it.

• Define the problem in relationship terms. Is it one that all concerned see as a problem and want to resolve, or is it an individual need? If the problem affects more than one person, then all involved need to work on the solution.

• Identify how each person contributes to the problem. Because the family is a system, if *we* have a problem, I must be doing something that helps maintain it. Identifying how each person contributes to a problem helps the family know what behaviors need to be changed to resolve the problem.

• State the goal in terms of behaviors you want to increase or decrease. No fair saying, "We want a better family— that's our goal." It's too vague. What can you and others do to have a better family? What will change in order for your family to be "better"? Be specific.

• Generate alternative solutions. Here is where you brainstorm new ideas. What specific things might be considered in working toward a solution?

• Evaluate alternative solutions. Evaluation should include two elements: Will it achieve the goal and solve the problem? Is it consistent with my values and resources?

• Select the best solution. After creating and evaluating various solutions, it is then necessary to determine the specifics—who will do what, when, where, and how often.

This step is important in maintaining clear family communication.

• Implement the solution. Try the solution long enough to determine whether it will or will not work. Remember, change is not easy. It requires considerable effort, but the rewards are significant.

• Evaluate your progress. Ask yourself three questions: Did we do what we agreed to do? Did it achieve our goals? If not, what went wrong? If the goal was not achieved, go back to the beginning of this section and begin the process again.[4]

Strong families have hammered out effective ways of solving problems. Most of them implement the steps mentioned above in some way. Another excellent source I have found for conflict resolution is a book by James G. T. Fairfield called *When You Don't Agree: A Guide to Resolving Marriage and Family Conflicts* (Herald Press, 1977). You will find several excellent suggestions by this Christian author that will enhance your family communication.

Individual Responsibility Assumed

Have you ever noticed that in troubled families there are always experts on what's wrong—with the other people? I remember on one occasion I was counseling with a couple who were very intent on telling me all their "war stories." The husband saw quite clearly all the faults of his wife, and her "insight" into his problems was equally as forceful. After listening to the harangue for several minutes (and wishing I had worn my striped shirt and whistle), I said to the husband, "Tell me, what are you contributing to the problem in your marriage?" Silence. Stunned silence. That question did not compute. While he was more than ready to point out to me his wife's faults, he was not in touch with his own at all. He finally responded, "Well, I'm sure I'm to blame at times, but she . . ." and off he went again on another round of criticism.

In counseling couples and families, I have learned to look for those critical turning points, where I can see regression turn to progression. One of the most critical turning points is when the family members involved stop blaming someone else for their predicament and start assuming their own responsibility for it. In a family system everybody has a part, and no one is immune from or outside that process. Strong families are those who are willing to assume individual responsibility and who work on their *own* lives, rather than chasing after "specks of sawdust" in other people's lives (see Matt. 7:3-5).

Time Spent Communicating

So much of the total message is nonverbal that a big chunk of it is missed when we don't see one another while the message is being conveyed. That's why the eyes are about as important as the ears when it comes to communicating. That's why your mother, when she was angry and wanted to get a clear message across, put her hand on your shoulder or chin and said, "Look at me when I talk to you!" And you looked!

Strong families have a variety of ways of arranging for "talk time," but they all manage to do it somehow. Perhaps it's at the breakfast table or dinner table, or a set family time, or periodic specially called meetings. The frequency and the mode change, but they realize that family communication is the life blood of their relationship. And so they make time for it.

We will examine in more detail in the next chapter the importance of families spending time together. It deserves mention here in the context of family communication because it is impossible to communicate effectively if family members don't set aside time to be together eyeball-to-eyeball.

Active Listening

For communication to work, somebody has to be listening. Most of us would rather be talking. Listening is by far the most difficult element in the communication process. By "active" listening, I mean that we concentrate our full attention on the one doing the speaking. A lot of our family communication is in transit—either while we are doing some activity, on our way through a room in the house, or from another room. To listen actively means to look at the person who is speaking and to absorb the total message beyond the mere content. Since we all can listen several times faster than we can speak, our ever-present tendency is to let our minds wander from the speaker instead of concentrating on the total message.

James Fairfield suggests six skills by which we can improve our listening and perceiving:[5]

• Concentrate on the present. Resist the temptation to "read in" past experiences that color present interpretations. The present meaning is your focus.

• Defuse the message. Some words will trigger an emotional response in you that may not be the speaker's intent. Try to understand *their* meaning instead of reading in your own.

• Slow your evaluation. Hear the other person out, particularly if you disagree with him or her. By working through your own expectations, you will keep from prejudging the emotional level of the other's statements. Don't make up your mind prematurely.

• Sift the irrelevant. Particularly in a conflict, we tend to elaborate. By sifting out the irrelevant detours, we will be able to focus on the real issue at hand without getting sidetracked.

• Check the message. No need to doubt what the speaker said. You can say, "Here's what I heard you say," then repeat the message in condensed form, and ask, "Is that right?" Be sure that you convey accurate understanding and not approval or disapproval.

• Register acceptance and empathy. You can show your acceptance of the message—"I see what you mean," or "I understand what you're saying"—without necessarily agreeing with it or giving up your own convictions. Empathetic understanding wants to try to feel as the speaker feels, to see things from his or her perspective.

It is impossible to listen and at the same time formulate a response. Many have tried, but it can't be done. Listening is too important in our families to mix it with anything else. It conveys respect and value.

Positive Communication Patterns
Every family develops various patterns of communication that are predictable and repeatable. Most of us are unaware of these patterns to a great extent. My challenge to you is to spend some time figuring out what those patterns are. If you were to characterize the percentage of positive to negative communication, what would it be? In strong families the positive will far outweigh the negative.

These communication patterns, whether positive or negative, are learned and they can be changed. If nagging and criticism are part of your home atmosphere, you can change when you make up your mind to do so. And you don't even have to wait for everybody else to change. Positive communication is contagious.

If you as a parent have a problem of continually criticizing your children, check your expectations of them. They may not be realistic and attainable and may require some adjustment. The problem with some kids is that they act like kids, when we want to impose adult standards of behavior on them.

Criticism, faultfinding, and nagging rarely accomplish their desired ends. What they do accomplish is lower self-esteem, and a lack of respect and acceptance. Strong family communication patterns will emphasize things that "build each other up" and "encourage one another" (1 Thes. 5:11).

Focus on Intent, Not Just Content

Few, if any, of us say exactly what we mean when we communicate. We sometimes conclude in exasperation, "Oh, well, you know what I mean." Words are sometimes poor vehicles to convey what we really mean.

Healthy families seem to develop a sense of picking up on the meaning and intent of communication with one another. That quality is no doubt a combination of developed sensitivity, time spent in talking and listening to one another in a warm, accepting environment, and a good track record of checking out past messages and meanings.

I am reminded of the joke about the man who came across an old acquaintance he had not seen for quite awhile. After exchanging greetings the man inquired about his friend's wife. "How's Martha doing?" The friend replied, "She's no longer with me; she's in heaven." "I'm sorry," the startled man said. Realizing that was not an appropriate answer to the wife's celestial state, he exclaimed, "I'm glad." That didn't have a good ring to it, either, so in total frustration he said, "Well, I'm surprised!"

You and I know what the guy meant, in searching for an appropriate answer to his friend's circumstances. I'm glad that I have friends and family who are willing at times to wade through my muddled messages and discover my real meaning and intent. I'm also thankful for a God who without fail hears my heart, even when the words don't match.

Acknowledgment of What Others Say

Have you ever watched families who did not acknowledge the messages of their members? Dr. Jerry Lewis, a psychiatrist who has done considerable research and writing on healthy families, describes them.

In many families, when any member speaks or gives some sign, the others respond—with words, a smile, a shrug—but the speaker knows that he or she has been heard and his or her message is acknowledged. If a family is impervious, it may have a very crushing impact upon the individual whose statements are ignored.[6]

Not to look, to touch, or in any way to recognize someone is even alive and present in a family is to invite serious self-worth problems for the person who is so treated.

It's a great feeling of security to know that in my family I am free to say what I wish and it will be acknowledged. Everyone might not agree, but all agree to my right to speak and to be heard.

Informal and Spontaneous Conversational Style

My observation of strong families has convinced me that there is a high level of spontaneity in the communication style. At times, it might be mistaken by an outsider as confusion. But despite the appearance, the meaning is clear.

Some communications experts say that interrupting while another is speaking always conveys disrespect for the speaker. However, in Lewis' study of healthy families, he found frequent interruptions in their conversational styles.[7] No disrespect was intended or implied, and everyone got equal treatment. The key seems to lie in the spirit of the interrupter and the intent of the action.

Troubled families will have more difficulty shifting from the more formal, stilted style of conversation to the freewheeling variety than healthy families will. The functional ones seem to have the ability to select the style most appropriate to the occasion.

Sense of Humor

Surely one of God's good gifts to his creatures is the ability to laugh, to see humor, to enjoy something funny. As I look at God's creation, I am convinced He has a sense of humor (monkeys are my favorite humorists of nature). Jesus certainly had more of a sense of humor than we usually give Him credit for, as time after time He used humorous circumstances to teach great lessons (see Matt. 7:3-5).

Stress experts are telling us about the therapeutic effects of laughter in the relieving of tension. I love the times when our family gets the "crazies" or goes "bananas," as we sometimes refer to it. I like gag gifts and jokes played—even on me. When you come down to it, we human beings are pretty funny creatures. Humor is the gift of God that keeps us from taking ourselves too seriously.

Of course, humor should never be at the expense of another's misfortune or hurt. Tragedy and comedy are never quite as far apart as we sometimes believe them to be. Blessed is the person whose sense of humor is tempered with sensitivity and appropriateness. In the words of the wise man, "A cheerful heart is good medicine" (Prov. 17:22).

Flexible Communication Patterns

This characteristic has been touched on under other headings. But its importance demands that it be listed separately. Flexibility implies that the communication process can change according to circumstantial needs.

The distinguishing mark I see between the verbal patterns of troubled families and those of healthy ones is the ability to be flexible and to change. Troubled families will tend to have one main conversational style, regardless of the situation. On the other hand, strong families know that time and circumstances change and they must change with them. Parental conversational styles with children change from supervisor and tutor to that of friends as they grow into adulthood. On other occasions, there is "a time to be silent and a time to speak," as Solomon reminds us (Ecc. 3:7). These strong families have a sense of timing and appropriateness that helps them to view change and flexibility as friends instead of enemies.

Where Does It All Start?

What or who is the key to the development of healthy family communication patterns? All the family life experts agree on this one. *The adults in the family set the tone for the entire family.* In most American families, that is the parents—the husband and wife. But the principle holds equally true in single-parent families. Children will key off the significant adults in their lives, and especially their parents. The relationship that spouses have (even in circumstances of separation and divorce) will have a marked effect on the parent-child communications.

Let me single out the married couples with children living at home. The quality of your marriage will directly influence your relationship with your children. They will learn how to resolve conflict, how to deal with anger and frustration, how to express emotions, and a thousand other things *from you*. They are learning, whether you want to be teaching them or not.

Since the husband-wife relationship is so pivotal, doesn't it make a lot of sense to spend time evaluating that relationship and working on it and spending time with it? This inevitable learning our children do from us can be seen as a threat or a great blessing. God designed for kids to be influenced by their parents. But He intends for parents to invest some time and energy and resources into keeping their own relationship alive and vibrant and beautiful.

Trouble with the children doesn't invariably mean trouble between husband and wife. But most of the time there is more of a direct connection than we think. This statement is not intended to produce a guilt trip. It is a simple statement of how people function in the system we call a family. Parents set the tone for the entire family process.

Improving Family Communication

One of the keys to improvement is an increased awareness of your family communication patterns. The following twenty questions will be helpful in finding out where you are and what needs changing. Each family member may write out the answers or give them orally.

1. How do your family members talk to you?
2. How do they talk to one another?
3. How does what you say affect what they say?
4. How does what they think about affect what you say?
5. Which member of your family talks the least?
6. Which member of your family talks the most?
7. Which member talks first?
8. Which member talks last?
9. Who doesn't talk unless asked to talk?
10. Who tends to attack what others say?
11. Who uses the harshest words?
12. Who asks the most questions?
13. Who talks more about facts?
14. Who talks more about feelings?
15. Who doesn't talk on a feeling level?
16. Who dominates the conversation?
17. How does your family resolve conflicts?
18. Is your communication pattern mainly positive or negative? What percentage of each?
19. Is everyone free to say what he or she feels?
20. If you were going to give your family a grade for its overall communication style, what would it be?[8]

Footnotes

1. Salvador Minuchin, *Families and Family Therapy* (Cambridge: Harvard University Press, 1974), p. 47.

2. H. Norman Wright, *Communication and Conflict Resolution in Marriage* (Elgin, Ill.: David C. Cook, 1977), p. 6.

3. Wright, *The Family That Listens* (Wheaton, Ill.: Victor Books, 1978), pp. 107-108.

4. "People-helping" workbook. Privately printed. Adapted from Jan Harrell and Bernard Gurney, "Training Married Couples in Conflict Negotiation Skills," in David H. L. Olson (Ed.), *Treating Relationships* (Lake Mills, Iowa: Graphic Publishing Co., 1976), pp. 154-157.

5. James G. T. Fairfield, *When You Don't Agree: A Guide to Resolving Marriage and Family Conflicts* (Scottdale, Penn.: Herald Press, 1977), pp. 83-87.

6. Jerry M. Lewis, *How's Your Family? A Guide to Identifying Your Family's Strengths and Weaknesses* (New York: Brunner/Mazel, 1979), p. 58.

7. *Ibid.*

8. Adapted from H. Norman Wright, *The Family That Listens*, pp. 66-67.

4
Spending Time Together

*A*s I consider all these positive qualities of healthy families, I am struck by the fact that they are so interrelated and interdependent. Nowhere is this more true than in the matter of spending time together. It's difficult to express appreciation to people you seldom see. Certainly communication is hindered. All the other traits that follow are damaged considerably if there is no time spent together as a family.

Dolores Curran, in her excellent book, *Traits of a Healthy Family*, says that lack of time might be the most pervasive enemy the healthy family has.[1] That is certainly true in my own family. Dr. James Dobson says that he doesn't know any families that aren't overcommitted.[2] What a struggle! About the time we feel we are making progress, something else comes along and complicates things all over again.

My two daughters used to have pet gerbils. I loathe the little creatures—they are still nothing but rats to me. But on occasion I found myself watching them. They were hyper, going about chewing up paper and whatever else gerbils do with great frenzy, as if there were no tomorrow. Then it hit me—that's the way I act at times. Those little creatures I had no use for were mirroring my hectic lifestyle. Come to think of it, some of the things I was doing were probably about as useless as what they were doing.

Spending meaningful time together involves a constant struggle, for it is never as easy as we think it was for families in the past. But there is hope. There are some families who are swimming successfully against the currents of our culture, carving out of a busy schedule some quality time together. My goal in this chapter is to address the problem of spending time together in a realistic way, not to produce guilt trips. What we need are practical suggestions for achieving some sense of balance in our families.

Clarification and Revelation

Before we look at those practical suggestions, there are a couple of areas that need some attention. The first has to do with our definition of family togetherness. Is togetherness always desirable? Can there be too much of it? How can the members of a family exercise a strong degree of togetherness and at the same time develop a healthy sense of individuality? Just what is this "spending time together" that we are talking about?

David Olson is a specialist in family studies research who is doing some significant work on helping us understand how families function. He identifies two key concepts that determine a family's condition—their degree of cohesion and their degree of adaptability. The degree of cohesion, or togetherness, can range all the way from disengaged—low cohesion, to enmeshed—high cohesion. The degree of family adaptability, of flexibility, can be characterized by a rigidity—low adaptability, on one extreme, all the way to chaotic—high adaptability. His point is that a balance must be achieved in both areas for families to function properly. Extremes should be avoided.[3]

While Dr. Jerry Lewis recognizes the need for regular together times for families, he also stresses the development of autonomy, particularly among the children. Families are made up of individuals who do not have to sacrifice that individuality. Lewis labels the production of truly autonomous children one of the most important jobs of the modern family.

> Autonomy is based upon an individual's sense of separateness—the understanding that no matter how close one feels to others, how connected to family, spouse, or friends, how much like others one may be—there is a fundamental individuality present. Beyond experiencing one's self as separate from others, autonomy involves the capacity to function independently. An individual may sense his or her separateness, but rely so intensely on others that independent functioning is impossible. Autonomy involves both separateness and the ability to function on one's own. The autonomous person is able to separate his or her feelings and thoughts from those of others. "I feel . . ." or "I think . . ." is often used in conversation. Finally, the autonomous person is able to initiate activities rather than only responding to the behavior of others.[4]

As I am emphasizing the necessity of family time together, I am not doing so at the expense of destroying individuality for the sake of the group. This togetherness is not a smothering or forced kind. Togetherness is not an attempt to clone. Rather, it is a natural, enjoyed experience. Good families enjoy being together!

The other area that needs our attention before exploring some practical suggestions for spending time together is the biblical foundation for this characteristic. Implied throughout the Bible is the idea that parents should be the trainers of their children in moral, ethical, and spiritual development. But nowhere is it more beautifully exemplified than in Moses' admonition in Deuteronomy 6:4-9. Moses had just reminded God's people of old about the heart of His will, the Ten Commandments. He then gave what was to be called by Jesus the Greatest Commandment, followed by instructions on how to teach God's will to future generations:

> Hear, O Israel: The Lord our God, the Lord is one. Love the Lord your God with all your heart and with all your soul and with all your strength. These commandments that I give you today are to be upon your hearts. Impress them on your children. Talk about them when you sit at home and when you walk along the road, when you lie down and when you get up. Tie them as symbols on your hands and bind them on your foreheads. Write them on the doorframes of your houses and on your gates.

Even after the cultural and chronological jumps are made to our contemporary times, one message stands out as clear as day: *in order to teach our children in the way of the Lord, we are going to have to spend some time together.* If it is true, as I believe, that many of our values and beliefs are caught more than taught, the imperative of being together is even more essential. When we are spending time together as a Christian family, we are doing God's will. We talk with our children about what is important to us when we're in the car together, when we're in the yard, when we're in the house— with the TV off, at mealtime, and at bedtime. What a privilege God has entrusted to us as parents—to mold young lives in such a meaningful way!

Working on Spending Time Together

The word *working* is chosen advisedly because our family times will not come naturally. They only come through effort and planning. Following are some things I am finding helpful in the daily battle with time. Even though I may lose some battles with time along the way, my hope is that I will eventually win the war. The victory for me will be a wife and children who feel that I love them enough to put time with them above all other human relationships.

• Prioritize! Prioritize! Prioritize! I wish it were so that in a moment of reflection I could once for all evaluate my priorities and then set my face steadfastly toward the goal. Wouldn't that be nice? But it just doesn't work that way. As I have already indicated, for me it is a daily struggle. To be sure, I have overall goals and priorities that remain essentially unchanged—some are not even negotiable for me. But the practical living out of those aims is quite another thing. Sometimes the fog sets in and I lose sight of the goal.

So on occasion, I have to sit down and prioritize what I am doing, where I am spending my time, what is really important. One matter of particular concern to me is the amount and quality of time spent with Pam, Alison, and Jennifer. I am aware of the danger that some Christian writers are now warning us about—making an idol out of the family. Too much attention to family to the exclusion of other relationships is not only unhealthy but is also unchristian. "The family turned in on itself" is not a solution, for it only complicates matters more. I am aware of the words of Jesus about putting Him and His cause above family concerns. But does that mean that to be a good Christian, my family relationships have to suffer? I think not. For most people, the call to discipleship does not entail such a sacrifice. Rather, I see Christian family relationships suffering more from pursuit after materialism and prominence and selfishness than from discipleship. I understand God to be saying that we as Christians have a relationship and responsibility to those of our family that we have to no one else. The family is the laboratory of Christian living. If Christianity doesn't work in the home, where does it work? Our family relationships should not take on the status of a sacred cow, to be sure. But they *are* sacred, nevertheless. Our priorities ought to reflect that sacredness.

• Monitor your level of involvement in organized activities, especially those involving the children. "Get involved!" Is that good advice? Sometimes it is and sometimes it isn't. From the viewpoint of effect on family life, overinvolvement in organized activities seems to be a far greater problem than underinvolvement. If mothers put a taximeter on the family car and charged the going rate to haul children to their extracurricular activities, they would be independently wealthy before long! For the kids it's Little League, soccer, scouts, band, or two dozen other things. For the parents, the list is almost as long.

I used to be a big fan of organized sports for kids. But frankly, I have become increasingly disenchanted, primarily because of the alarming control they have over family life. Practices and game schedules interfere with family meals, church activities, and leisure time, not to mention weekends and vacations. And the intensity and dedication demanded of these kids (more for the sake of coaches and parents than for the kids) is staggering. Certainly some good qualities are taught in these experiences, but at what price? I really resent the control that outside people have over my family life, at least to the degree many of them demand.

The church is not immune from the organized activity trap. At the Highland Church where I am presently a family minister, we have gone in recent years to more and more organized activities involving the entire family. We have two family retreats a year, and for many of us, they are some of the most memorable experiences we have shared. Of course, our children need some organized peer group activities, but maybe not as many as we are accustomed to having, and not as expensive as some of them are.

The point is that organized activities are good for family members, but they must be limited. When they call for an inordinate sacrifice of family time, whether on the part of parents or children, they need to be limited.

• Control your work schedule. I realize that about half the married women reading this book will have some type of job outside the home. While women certainly do struggle to control their work schedules, it is to the men that I want to speak here. We men are by far the greatest offenders in choosing not to control our work. My purpose here is not to go into all the underlying reasons why men overcommit themselves to their work. They range all the way from enjoying it too much, to workaholism, to escape from self. Whatever the reasons, the refusal to control our work schedules can wreak havoc with our family time together.

I use the phrase *"choosing* not to control our work" purposefully. Granted, in some professions there is more choice than in others; but in *all* of them, we have more choice than we think. I know physicians who have a great family life and I know those whose family commitments are disastrous. I know military people with high priority for family time and those with practically none. I know ministers who spend quality time with their families, and I know some who spend most of their time saving other families and lose their own in the process.

We need to take a hard look at what is required of our middle and upper-management people in terms of their job demands taking priority over their family. A growing number of men who love their families are saying no to promotions that mean relocation, in order to put their family needs first. Sometimes it even means making a job change and earning less money. I really admire men who have decided to control their work schedule, rather than let it control them.

• Develop a family "philosophy" of leisure and together time, allowing for some individual differences. What does your family like to do when there is leisure time? Families are unique. What one family dearly loves to do, another is not the least interested in. And even within families, differences about leisure exist. I think of my own family. One of the things we all like to do is travel. But as we travel, we all want to do different things. Pam likes to go to antique and junk stores (there is a difference); Alison and Jennifer like to swim; I like to take naps and restful walks, and do things that require very little brain power. On most trips, each of us gets something of what we want individually, but still we're together a lot.

I have found it advantageous to schedule some of our trips around my speaking schedule. Whenever possible, I take all or part of my family with me. We have been able to go places and see things we would not otherwise have experienced. For some families, the blending of business and pleasure is not a workable alternative.

The philosophy of leisure I am advocating does not extend just to out-of-town trips and vacations. Of more importance is the family's attitude toward the day-to-day times the family is together. Talk it over. Have a family conference. What would each member like to have happen when the family is together? How can you develop a spirit of give-and-take to where individual preferences do not constantly work against the gathered times? Make your goals realistic, considering your own unique family situation. Impossible standards only serve to frustrate the situation more.

We tried an experiment recently. For two months, we turned off the television. It did wonders for our family life! We talked more, read more, and played together more than we ever had in recent years. With rare exceptions, I believe that family time around the TV is mostly wasted. Dolores Curran found that the stronger families were, the less TV they watched.[5] Do you think there could be any connection?

• Commit to regular family times together. I admire families who seem to have it all together when it comes to scheduling special times for them to be with one another. "Every Monday night we have family time, no matter what," a friend told me. Since I've promised you that I would be realistic and honest, I must say that this type of rigid routine is hard for me to sustain. My several attempts through the years to become more systematic with our family times are silent testimonies to my failure.

Yet, let me hasten to add that there is tremendous value in special times together that are planned ahead. I am convinced that they must be a part of a healthy Christian family life. The *way* those times are brought about, however, opens up several possibilities. For some families, the same night every week is workable. For others, the time will vary, perhaps being during the day on a weekend. Families with variable schedules may find it advantageous to sit down at the beginning of the month and determine their times together. Of course, the older the children, the more difficult the scheduling. But it's not impossible, so don't give up.

We'll talk more in a later chapter about the kind of things that can be done in the special family times. My purpose in this section is twofold. First, these times have to be planned. "Someday" or "as soon as" won't work. And don't get discouraged and give up when your plans are temporarily interrupted. Be flexible. Second, I firmly believe that in the dual parent family, the father should take the lead in working out the family times. A lot of Christian mothers do it by default, but it is much better for Dad to assume that responsibility.

• Don't do everything together, but do *something* together. The family that does *everything* together is called an *enmeshed family*. We have learned from David Olson that enmeshment is an unhealthy extreme of togetherness, where family members move together like a covey of quail. Where you see one, you usually see them all. They are virtually inseparable. The parents are never away from the kids for more than minutes. What a tragedy for both the children and the parents!

The danger in enmeshment comes when the children try to exert their individuality and autonomy. Many of them have great difficulty in pulling away from their family of origin and beginning one of their own. So, when I speak of family togetherness, I am not referring to enmeshment where individuality is not accepted.

On the other hand, the *disengaged family* rarely does anything together. They have taken autonomy and individuality too far, at the expense of family unity. I encourage these families to do *something* together.

Together does not imply that every single member of the family has to be present. For instance, there are activities that each of my daughters and I enjoy. Alison and I like to play tennis. Jennifer and I go for bike rides or attend sporting events. Alison and Pam like to go shopping. These are healthy coalitions within the family unit, revolving around shared interests. Unhealthy coalitions, where two people take sides or purposefully exclude others who want to be involved, can really be detrimental to family unity.

• Be prepared to meet resistance. Anything worthwhile will be resisted by someone, and spending time together is no exception. The resistance will come primarily from two sources. First, it may come from those outside your family. For your time together to become a reality, you will have to prioritize your activities and involvement. That means selection and control, and may involve elimination of organized activities.

Some of the people you turn down will understand, but others will not. Particularly difficult are decisions about worthy activities, such as those of a church and community nature. The push in our culture is toward more involvement, more fragmentation of family life. Those who are pushing for this will not understand your choices.

The second area of resistance may come from within your family. You may notice it particularly from older children, if they do not have a long-standing positive experience of family times together. While it's easier to begin on a regular basis when the children are young, it is not impossible, by any means, to start when they're older. But it does require from the parents an *ability to listen respectfully* to their children in gaining ideas for activities, and a *flexibility* that enables them to find something that would be enjoyable for all. Perhaps shorter times spent with each older child would be a good way to begin.

• Slow down and live! That's what the traffic signs say. And it's pretty good advice for a family lifestyle as well. Have you ever stopped in the middle of a hectic day and asked yourself, "What am I doing in this gerbil cage? Why am I killing myself like this?" I certainly have. That reflection can be the beginning of a good healthy evaluation of who we are and why we're here and what we're supposed to be doing.

On one occasion, Jesus advised some rest and solitude for His disciples, after a rather hectic time of ministry. "And He said unto them, 'Come ye yourselves apart into a desert place, and rest a while'; for there were many coming and going, and they had no leisure so much as to eat" (Mark 6:31, KJV).

I think some of what Jesus is saying here is, "Come apart or you will 'come apart.' " For me, time spent with family members who love me and accept me and respect me helps as much as anything I know to keep me from coming apart. Maybe it will work for you too.

Balance Is the Key

I hope you hear that theme flowing through this chapter. So often our choices as to how we spend our time are not between good ones and bad ones. They are all good. But at closer examination, some are better than others. And once in awhile, one that is clearly best comes along.

The balance lies in knowing the degree of togetherness or separateness needed in our families for quality relationships. I am convinced that the solution to a more fulfilling family life together lies *within* the family, not outside. No new program or concept is going to come along and rescue the family that is losing its unifying force. But parents, by using these suggestions as a starting point, can make progress in capturing that sense of joy that so many people want and too few have—a family that enjoys spending time together.

Footnotes

1. Dolores Curran, *Traits of a Healthy Family* (Minneapolis: Winston Press, 1983), p. 120.
2. James Dobson, "How to Save Your Marriage," in *Focus on the Family*. (Waco, Texas: Word, Inc., 1978), Tape 3.
3. David Olson, et al., "Circumplex Model of Marital and Family Systems I: Cohesion and Adaptability Dimensions, Family Types, and Clinical Applications," *Family Process*, 1979, pp. 3-28. Olson and his associates have developed an excellent assessment tool for pre-marriage testing and marriage enrichment. For information write Prepare-Enrich, P.O. Box 190, Minneapolis, Minn. 55440.
4. Jerry M. Lewis, *How's Your Family? A Guide to Identifying Your Family's Strengths and Weaknesses* (New York: Brunner/Mazel, 1979), pp. 64-65.
5. Dolores Curran, *Traits of a Healthy Family*, pp. 36-39, 161-162.

5
Cultivating Commitment

C ommitment is a word that has fallen on hard times lately. You don't even find it used much. Commitment—being obligated or bound by a conviction—is a declaration of association brought on by a conscious moral choice. And then there's the really scary term, "total commitment," bantered about all too carelessly by some religious zealots who dare to think that the ideal is consistently attainable. Even our "total commitment" isn't always total.

Commitment to the family is the fourth of the six characteristics that were found to be present in strong families. In a world that is hesitant to commit to much of anything, this quality stands out, arousing our curiosity. What is it that fosters loyalty and cohesion in these people? What is it that causes them to be committed to promoting each other's happiness and welfare? The answers do not come with a great deal of ease. Not a lot of research has been done in the area of family commitment, but I believe we can discover some of the secrets.

Ingredients of Family Commitment

Commitment, like happiness, is more a by-product of other qualities than an end in itself. One cannot simply decide to be "more committed" to family relationships. The decision must be accompanied by action. It is the development of certain qualities in the family relationship that produces commitment. I have isolated twelve key concepts that form the essential ingredients of family commitment. No doubt you can add more. But at least the ones mentioned here need to be present to some degree for there to be a climate of positive growth toward mutual commitment.

• Respect. Like Rodney Dangerfield, some families "don't get no respect." Dolores Curran, in listing respect as one of the major traits of a healthy family, reports that family members usually all have respect for people or none of them do. Rarely are they mixed.[1] That's interesting, isn't it. Apparently, respect is either taught, modeled, and accomplished by the parents, or it isn't. Let's look at respect in its various forms.

Self-respect is the beginning point. It's hard to show respect for others when we habor disrespect for our own selves. The beauty of the Christian faith is that self-respect is a gift of God, given through His grace. It cannot be earned by our efforts at "proper" behavior.

An outgrowth of self-respect is the mutual respect shown in our families. That quality can be demonstrated in several ways. It can be shown in respect for individual differences, without making people feel strange or rejected. In the relationship between generations lie a number of potential hindrances to mutual respect. For instance, I think of some parents who respect other adults reasonably well, but who don't respect their own children. They treat them as half-persons at best. Biblical admonitions on how to get along with others and treat them with respect and dignity do not carry a disclaimer—"Not applicable in the case of parent-child relationships." Children are people too! Then I think of children who do not show proper respect for their parents, particularly in their conversations with them. Healthy families simply do not tolerate disrespect in any family relationship.[2] Disagreement, yes. Disrespect, no.

Of course, the respect shown in the family can also be seen in the way members show respect to those outside the family. Teachers and law enforcement people are saying loud and clear that America's children on the whole have a shocking lack of respect for the personhood and property of others. The really strong families stand out in contrast. They are the ones who are helping others and getting involved with those in need. Underneath it all is a basic respect for self, family, and others. A person is not likely to get any respect until he begins to show it.

• Trust. It doesn't take long in observing a family's interaction for me to know something about their level of mutual trust. I can tell by the tone of voice and their general treatment of each other, as well as by the content of the messages. Healthy families can be trusting in their relationships because they have learned to be secure in sharing their individual thoughts and feelings. Just as in the matter of respect, trust is likely to be present at all levels of human encounter, or not present in any of them. Trust provides openness in a family, and openness is an integral factor in the development of family commitment.

Family trust is delicate in that when it is broken, it may not easily and quickly be replaced. But the good news is that it can be built back with effort. Strong families have a way of giving each other another chance when trust is violated. In families, the tone of trust is set by the parents in their own relationship. It's easy to be committed to a family who trusts.

• Acceptance. We had a saying in central Texas, where I grew up, that the old-timers used to repeat: "Orta ain't is." That needs some translating. A liberal rendering into plain

English is, "What ought to be is not the way it is." At times I know the way things ought to be in my life and others' lives, but that is not the way they are. Some troubled families get their "orta" and their "is" mixed up. They deal with one another in "oughts" and "shoulds," all the time failing to accept the person as he or she is. In healthy families, the matter of personal acceptance is not in question. They may on occasion judge a person's behavior as unacceptable, but never the person. I believe it's easy to develop loyalty and commitment to a family that accepts me, no matter what. Come to think of it, that's certainly the way my heavenly Father treats me all the time!

• Goals. It may sound a bit strange to list goals as an ingredient of commitment. But on closer reflection, I hope it makes a lot of sense to you. It is a common tendency to neglect what we do not plan. That's true for me in a number of areas of my life. So it is in the family. If we do not have clear-cut goals and plans that show direction and purpose, we are likely to get sidetracked. The result will be that forces will be activated to pull us away from a mutual commitment to each other. Goals mutually shared tend to unite families in a common commitment.

• Affirmation. "Strokes," "warm fuzzies," whatever you call them, everybody needs them. We've already seen how healthy families constantly affirm one another. When mutual affirmation is seen in the light of developing family commitment, the need is even more obvious. I am going to feel a great loyalty and positive pull toward a group of people who are continually affirming me as a person. To know that I am appreciated, not just for what I produce, but for who I am, causes the roots of commitment to these people to run deep. Affirmations say, "I care" and "You count." It's hard to turn your back on that kind of message.

• Unselfishness. At a funeral for an older woman, the minister used a phrase that fits our discussion here. He was talking about how the husband had served his ailing wife for a number of years and referred to it as "unselfish devotion." Maybe there's a hint of redundancy in the phrase, but I know exactly what the minister meant. Devotion or commitment, if you please, has at its very core an unselfish spirit. I think of my own mother and father who have given unselfishly to so many in their family. That to which we give ourselves has a way of demanding our loyalty. I imagine that a selfish spirit breaks up as many families as anything else I know. Surely if selfishness breaks families apart, an unselfish spirit binds them together. I know of nothing more close to the heart of God Himself than unselfish giving to others. At no time are we more like the Lord than when we are giving unselfishly of ourselves.

• Responsibility. You mothers are probably going to be all in favor of this one! "This is where he lets our kids have it and straightens our husbands out for leaving clothes all over and for not helping around the house!" Well, that's certainly a part of responsibility. But there are other matters I want to discuss. As a family therapist, when I see continual shirking of responsibility in a family, I nearly always find it being unconsciously rewarded and sustained by the controlling adult(s) in the family. So, look at the way you *respond* to irresponsibility for a clue as to how to stop it. The guilty offenders apparently believe it's more rewarding to be irresponsible than to be responsible.

Responsibility produces self-respect. A person who is taught responsibility can feel confident because of the meaningful contributions to the family. Responsibility also implies involvement. One who is vitally involved in the family process is going to have a healthy commitment to other members of the family.

Another characteristic we have already mentioned really produces responsibility, and that is *respect*. We can only encourage responsibility in those we respect enough to have confidence in their ability. Notice a breakdown of the word *responsibility*—the ability to respond.

Family experts tell us that responsibility needs to be taught early in childhood. When it is not, the lesson is extremely difficult to learn in adulthood. Ted Moorehead elaborates on the far-reaching consequences:

> Mom doesn't really do the kids a favor by letting them get by with throwing their things around. And by not helping around the house. Dad doesn't build character by giving them everything they want. Too many children grow up without understanding the value of productive work and meeting obligations. Then they fail to make or carry out vital commitments. There is little inner discipline to their lives. They expect everything to be given like a prize, without effort or perserverance. In a tough spot, they give up with little struggle.[3]

• Understanding. I'm guessing that there are a lot of families out there whose members can say, "Nobody understands me." Close behind that complaint is another one, "Nobody listens to me." Listening is a key ingredient in understanding. I'm talking about a nonjudgmental, active kind of listening that takes effort and concentration, even when you may not like what you are hearing. Since it's impossible to listen with understanding and formulate a response in my mind at the same time, I need to concentrate first on understanding the message. Then I'll know better how to respond.

Do you think there's commitment in the family where all the members feel understood? (We're talking about understanding, not necessarily agreement.) I think so. The person who strives for understanding is able to pick up on the feelings, meanings, and needs of others. The person who feels understood also feels respected and valued and loved and very much a part of the family.

• Honesty. An elder in a church where I preached a number of years ago had a saying that sent fear through my bones. "Now, Brother Money," he would say, "let me be brutally frank." Every time he got "brutally frank" I knew I was headed for trouble. I found myself saying, "Please, whatever you do, don't be 'brutally frank!'" When I mention honesty, I am not talking about his style. When families take that brand of truth, significant damage results.

The spirit of honesty I am suggesting is best captured by Paul in Ephesians 4:15, where he encourages us to "speak the truth in love." They make a good pair—truth and love—and they should not be separated. It is also helpful if we deal more in facts and less in opinions and accusations. When describing feelings, we should use I-statements, owning up to our own feelings, rather than passing blame. Honesty in family relationships is a positive ingredient in the commitment process.

• Participation. It's hard for me to be committed to something of which I don't really feel a part. To be sure, the age of the children and the circumstances of the parent or parents determine to some degree the participation level of family members. Yet, the more balanced the interaction, the healthier the family usually is. In my work as a therapist, a problem I see in most troubled families is that somebody in the family feels left out. Unhealthy coalitions and alliances have been formed (usually by a parent and a child) that have caused other persons to feel a lack of participation in the group. The point is simply that when I participate, I feel as if I belong.

• Tradition. The story retold. The action repeated. This thing we call *tradition* is a strong force in family commitment. Edith Schaeffer talks about creating a "museum of memories" for children.[4] She even encourages the planning of memories and traditions for the family museum. Dolores Curran sums up the value of tradition well when she writes:

A sense of family means much more than the begats in the family Bible or the names on the homestead papers. A family's clanship embraces its legends, its characters, its history, its focal places and persons, its hospitality, its network, its deceased, its elderly, its babies, its traditions, and its rituals. The family who owns a rich sense of kinship is able to withstand stresses and disappointments that destroy other families. It's able to do so because its members have the support that comes from knowing they are not alone, either in the neighborhood or in history. It is in this kind of family that individuals are loved not for what they have or do but for who they are—members of the family.[5]

They don't seem like much at the time—"do your own thing" in the kitchen on Sunday evening meals, shrimp cocktails every Christmas Eve, and a thousand other little things. (A lot of our family traditions involve eating!) But that's a big part of what it means to be a family and to belong. There's a strange sort of security in that. The older I get, the more I cherish traditions and good memories. They give me a warm feeling and a sense of family.

• Religion. Since the next chapter will deal more specifically with this element, I will note the religious factor only in passing. My specific reason for listing it as an ingredient to commitment is that it has the capacity to be the glue that holds the family together, particularly in trying times. Being part of a religious tradition gives roots and a sense of continuity and support. The sharing of different religious traditions within a family doesn't mean the absence of commitment. In some instances, however, it may mean the weakening of family ties. Yet in deeply religious families, the factor of a shared faith will generally bind a family together.

Two Commitments
Let me make two suggestions as to the direction your commitment should take. First, *commit yourself to your marriage.*

While it is not possible for the readers who are single parents to do that, I'm sure they would join me in urging those of you who are married to recommit yourselves to each other. With a deep mutual commitment, many problems can be worked through successfully. People of lesser commitment would have given up on the same problems.

I have said it before—here it is again. The husband-wife relationship is the primary relationship in the family, by God's design. It sets the tone for the entire family interaction. Attention to this relationship supersedes the parent-child relationship, though neither need be neglected. That means time together *alone*—no kids and nobody else. Pam and I have made a practice of having a date two or three times a month ever since our older daughter was three weeks old. We even won the period of testing when they were small, of their crying and begging us not to leave. (The sitter would always say they stopped crying and began playing before we were out of the driveway.) Now, when things get a little testy between us, one of the girls will likely say, "Isn't it about time you two went out on a date?" They see the value in it, recognizing that things are better for everybody when they're good between us. And we love them for it.

The second admonition is like the first, except broader. *Commit your family to unconditional permanence.* I don't believe there is anything our girls could do that would cause us not to love them. The same is true of the relationship that Pam and I have with our parents. Now, somebody may not like what another person is doing, but the love is never in question.

It concerns me that some families I see—Christians included—tend to accept or reject their children, based on their performance or parental expectations or acceptable behavior. I think of that story called The Prodigal Son, in Luke 15, which should be called The Loving Father. The point of the parable is to show us that God is like that waiting father whose love for his son was great enough to let him go and strong enough to welcome him back. Of course, that's the story of our wanderings from God whose steadfast love never fails!

Unconditional love. Permanent love. Two words that capture the very essence of Christian *agape* love. "Our family will be here and love you and accept you, no matter what." I don't think many people give or receive that kind of family commitment. But you can.

Biblical Admonitions

The concept of family commitment is strong in the Bible. Let me mention briefly four Scriptures that come to mind. The first is one of the Ten Commandments, found in Exodus 20:12: "Honor your father and mother." That's not just for kids. As long as our parents live, we are to show honor through our treatment and care of them. In another vein, Jesus echoed an additional Mosaic passage when He reminded His listeners, in Matthew 19:6, of the permanent nature of the marriage commitment. The third instance, found in Mark 7:9-13, pictures Jesus debating with the Pharisees who, on the pretense of "giving to God," robbed their aging parents of the care they should have received from their adult children. Jesus said they nullified the Word of God by such action. Lastly, Paul admonished Timothy and his hearers, in 1 Timothy 5:3-4, to see that children and grandchildren of widows care properly for them. Paul had an interesting rationale for these offspring to care for one of their own: "These should learn first of all to put their religion into practice by caring for their own family and so repaying their parents and grandparents, for this is pleasing to God."

Heavy, isn't it. Apparently the Lord puts a pretty high premium on a deep commitment to the welfare of our families. But you know something? When the ingredients we have talked about are developed in your family and in mine, that type of family commitment—no matter what—will be a pleasure. Commitment, rather than being a burden, is truly one of God's most gracious blessings.

Footnotes

1. Dolores Curran, *Traits of a Healthy Family* (Minneapolis: Winston Press, 1983), p. 80.
2. For a discussion of ways to stop disrespect in children, see an article by Dr. Wayne Dyer, entitled, "Questions Women Ask Me," *Family Circle*, April 3, 1979.
3. Ted Moorehead, Jr., *How to be a Family and Survive* (Waco, Texas: Word Books, 1976), p. 32.
4. Edith Schaeffer, *What Is a Family?* (Old Tappan, N.J.: Fleming H. Revell Co., 1975), pp. 188ff.
5. Dolores Curran, *Traits of a Healthy Family*, p. 199.

6
Affirming Religious Values

*F*or a number of years we have known through research that there is a positive relationship of religion to marital happiness and successful family relationships. Stinnett's findings, then, are no great surprise. But the degree to which a religious core was found in these families is indeed encouraging. These findings don't necessarily mean that people who aren't religious cannot have happy marriages and good families. But the potential for satisfying family relationships is far greater among religiously oriented families than among those who do not share a faith. The alternative to faith in a transcendent God is faith in self. Our ailing society turned in on itself is testimony enough that the answers to life's perplexities do not lie within ourselves.

The research on strong families done by Stinnett, Curran, Lewis, and others was not limited to those in the Christian tradition. The *type* of religious conviction was not nearly the factor that the *presence* of that conviction was. However, in this instance, I am going to apply my comments to the Christian faith. Within that context lies the greatest potential for the wholeness and joy that so many families need today.

The Effect of Christian Qualities on the Family

If the Christian faith is passed on to our children, it will be because they see some direct benefit toward raising the quality of life together. Does it work? Does it make a difference in daily life? These are legitimate questions and worthy of our investigation. The strong Christian families who were studied—and the ones I know—answer an enthusiastic yes to those questions. Let's look at some of the Christian qualities that make a difference in their family life.

• Sense of purpose and meaning. Christianity is goal-oriented. It has a way of giving purpose. It helps to make and maintain meaning in life. The behavioral and social sciences fall woefully short here. In fact, it is not even their task. We all ask, "What does my existence mean? What is the purpose of living?" In the Bible the psalmists wrestled with these questions. The Books of Ecclesiastes and Job do, as do other writings. You and I wrestle with these questions. Our ultimate purpose as Christians is to glorify God. The depth and far-reaching implications of that statement are hard for me to fathom. But I believe faith in a transcendent God who loves me and who saves me gives me a lot of reason to live.

Few things we say or do will live forever. But what we teach our children about God and His plan for us can have eternal effects. Especially when we're down, stuck in the mire, experiencing a tragedy, or perhaps the death of a loved one—that is when we need a view of the big picture that God and His Word provide. We need to remember that what we see at the moment is not really the way it is, that there is more. Families who live in this kind of environment see their Christian faith as much more than an accepted set of beliefs. They see order and purpose and meaning that make a lot of difference in the way they live each day.

• Support and strength. Strong families usually attend church often and participate in religious activities together.

But the religious aspect goes deeper than just church activities. They are committed to a spiritual lifestyle that flows through every dimension of the family's relationship. They are able to draw strength and support from that lifestyle which provides a framework for their lives.

A Christian family can draw a lot of their support from the fellowship of the church. People who share a like faith can be of tremendous help in sharing burdens in a time of stress. When Christian families move, they are usually able to find a support system of new friends more quickly than relocating families who do not have church ties.

• Patience. When I think of patience, the prime examples in my life are my mother and father. I have a younger brother who is mentally retarded who has lived his entire life at home in their care. And oh, the patience they have had to exercise in that situation! If you were to ask them today about the development of that virtue, I think their response would be twofold. First, they would admit that they never thought of themselves as having all that much. Second, whatever patience they admitted having, they would credit the Lord with providing. I saw firsthand in my own family how two Christians, faced with a difficult and enduring situation, developed a virtue that is grounded in God's grace.

• Forgiveness. It is difficult for me to understand how people who are not Christians find it in their hearts to forgive others. Come to think of it, there are still some Christians who haven't quite mastered that virtue, either. Here's my point of reference. In my marriage and family counseling ministry, I have seen a number of couples who claimed no religious faith. As I would try to lead them to the point of granting mutual forgiveness in a strained relationship, I found it difficult to operate from their non-Christian frame of reference.

The Bible is the story of forgiveness—God's forgiveness

of man and man's forgiveness of his fellowman. When I deal with a Christian couple, at least I have the experience of their own forgiveness by God as a model to work from. In my own family relationships, when forgiveness is difficult for me but very much in order, I recall how the Lord treats me every day. Forgiveness comes easier when another has shown the way.

• Handling of anger. I hesitate to list this quality because there may still be some Christians who believe that the expression of anger is sinful, no matter what the circumstances. Ephesians 4:26 tells us that while anger has the potential for sin, it does not have to be so. Another lesson the passage teaches that is particularly applicable in a family context is that anger should be resolved quickly—"Do not let the sun go down while you are still angry." In our family, we have a rule that when one member is angry at another, he or she has about two days in which to talk that anger out. (I think we're still in the spirit of Ephesians 4:26.) When that rule is followed, anger never has an opportunity to turn into resentment and fester into bitterness and hatred.

• Positive attitudes. Even though we have already spent an entire chapter on mutual affirmation, which surely fosters positive attitudes, I want to mention it in this context. I know of no other single element in my own family life that has increased the quality of all our relationships more than a positive spirit toward each other. Positive breeds positive and negative breeds negative. There is no one alive and in their right mind who wouldn't rather be in a positive family environment than in a negative one. Here's another chance to get in my favorite verse, Ephesians 4:29: "Do not let any unwholesome talk come out of your mouths, but only what is helpful for building others up according to their needs, that it may benefit those who listen."

• Common values. The healthy Christian family functions from a definite set of values that has a moral base.

From this base comes a sense of right and wrong. We need that in order to make sense out of this world. Parents should not be ashamed to talk values with their children. I noticed lately in some literature I received from James Dobson that he suggested for parents to write down family values and encourage their children to commit them to memory. That may not be your way of doing it, but the teaching of values still needs to be done in some fashion. Of course, the Golden Rule is not a bad place to start. In a culture that is so self-centered, the value that cultivates a sensitivity to other people and serves their needs is right at the heart of the Christian faith.

Our list of practical qualities springing from Christianity, and having direct application to our families, could go on and on. The list could include other things we have already discussed, such as developing trust, respect for each other, a strong sense of family, and more. I hope that you see from the qualities mentioned that Christianity *does* work and *does* make a difference in daily life. I hope your children will see that through you.

Marks of a Strong Religious Family
When I think of all the great qualities that could be listed as we look at families with firm religious convictions, I realize that the list would be long and incomplete. There are so many things that could be mentioned here. So, with great restraint, I have decided to limit my discussion to five areas. Admittedly the list is selective, but I want to highlight those I think are central issues in building strong religious families.

• The strong family is sensitive to the various developmental stages of growth and faith its members go through. In my work with troubled families, I am amazed at how many of their problems center around unrealized developmental stages of life. I see the problem in parent-teen relationships more than anywhere else. Distraught parents are treating an adolescent the same way they treated him when he was eight years old. They have not learned the secret of gradually letting the child disengage from parental control, while at the same time nurturing the bonds of affection with the ever-changing child. Then when you throw in all the mid-life changes that many adults go through, it's enough to make the pot boil over. But the root problem is the parental failure to recognize developmental change—their children's and their own.

In the religious development of people, the same level of understanding is needed. Two authors in particular have addressed the issue of the growth of faith, building on the work of developmentalists like Lawrence Kohlberg, Erik Erikson, and others. John Westerhoff, in his book *Will Our Children Have Faith?* outlines four developmental levels of faith. The first is the experiential level (childhood faith); the second is the affiliative level (sense of belonging); the third is the searching level (testing of parents' belief); and the fourth is the owned faith (mature personal faith).[1] In a more thorough work, *Stages of Faith*, James Fowler presents six stages of faith development.[2] These men have made major contributions to our understanding of how faith grows in progressive and somewhat predictable stages. Family members—adults and children alike—will be at different levels in their religious development. As in all life-cycle phases, the more we understand about where we are and what is appropriate and natural at that stage, the better we are able to function as a family. The fear that often comes with family "religious crises" can be substantially reduced with that knowledge.

• The strong family practices its faith in some form constantly. Really, when you stop to think about it, we are all practicing our faith (or lack of it) all the time, whether we realize it or not. It cannot be otherwise. But my emphasis here is on living it and actualizing the faith through our actions. As I already mentioned, Stinnett found in his survey that the religious quality of these strong families went deeper than merely going to church and participating in religious activities. He said they were committed to a "spiritual lifestyle." That's my point here. In strong Christian families, their faith has a degree of concreteness and practicality through the practicing of the various qualities we have just talked about.

We have an excellent opportunity to teach our children that it is because of our faith that we take food to someone who is unable to cook, or receive a stranger into our home, or provide items for the needy. This type of approach catches the spirit of Deuteronomy 6:4-9 and the many other biblical passages that tie good works directly to the expression of our faith. We do what we do because of who we are—God's eyes and ears and hands and feet in a world that needs an *expressed* faith, more than a professed one.

• The strong family sees the church as a larger support system—a "greater" family. The modern family is searching for intimacy because of a sense of loneliness and isolation and a loss of history and tradition. All some families have is each other. This loss of a larger support system is taking its toll. Greater demands are placed on the parents for provision of the basic emotional needs for themselves and their children, with little outside help. The church is in an ideal position to counter this cultural trend by providing substitute families for the ones who are separated from their kin. The family needs the community life of the church to help bear the stresses brought on by contemporary society. Strong families plug into that source of social and spiritual strength that comes through the family of God.

I recall with great fondness the Christian people who have been family to us wherever we have lived. Our daughters have been blessed with several sets of grandparents throughout their life. Pam and I have brothers and sisters in Christ who are as dear to us as our own flesh and blood. What a great feeling to have that support and love of God's family wherever we go! I recently heard Dr. David Mace say that the church was in the greatest possible position to help lonely, confused people find a place of acceptance and belonging. I frankly wonder what people do in a time of need, when they don't have those spiritual family ties. Upon reflection, I do know what they do—they hurt.

• The strong family assumes its own responsibility for spiritual training, using the church as a supplement. Perhaps this point is offered as a balance to the previous one. While the church fills a critical need for mutual family support, I need to sound a warning against families depending on the institutional church for *too much* help. In section 2, I want to develop this theme in more detail. Suffice it to say at this point that we run a grave danger in assuming that it is the primary responsibility of the church to teach our children faith. The religious training of our children belongs primarily to the parents. That responsibility cannot be abdicated. The church can be a valuable supplement, one I would hate to do without. But if the job is not done, it will not be the church's fault.

Spiritual training through regular family times together is an excellent method. It provides an open, informal atmosphere where children can feel free to ask spiritual questions and discuss God's Word with their parents. When my daughters were preteens, every once in awhile we would have "Ask anything you want about the Bible" night. Believe me, they came up with some real questions. (Their questions were better than my answers!) In that time of struggling and learning and growing for all of us, we came closer to each other and to God. If you're interested in creative ideas to help you get started in a spiritual growth experience, I would suggest Wayne Rickerson's *Family Fun and Togetherness* and his more recent series on *Christian Family Activities*.[3]

• Strong families don't overreact when children test their faith or even reject it. Westerhoff and Fowler remind us of the developmental phase where inherited religion becomes one's own. It is a dangerous time for parents, because the child may reject their faith altogether. Notice that strong Christian families are not immune from this testing. Then strength lies in *how* they react during this period. More rigid parents, who hold themselves almost totally responsible for their grown children's lifelong faith, increase the pressure on their children. Rather than bringing them back into the fold, that move usually drives them further away. Another extreme measure is to disinherit the child, emotionally or financially. Such tactics only lead to more heartache on both sides.

The young person's temporary or "developmental" faith stance need not be mistaken for the eventual one, given time and the right environment. In fact, how the parents react to the faith-testing can be a decisive factor in where the adult child will eventually be in his or her faith pilgrimage. The best thing parents can do is to remain committed to their own faith.[4]

Affirming religious values is no easy task. There are a lot of variables, a lot of things out of parental control. And yet, I see good Christian families who are doing a great job of it. They inspire me and convince me that I can do it too, with a lot of help from the Lord and other Christians.

Footnotes

1. John H. Westerhoff, III, *Will Our Children Have Faith?* (New York: Seabury Press, 1976).

2. James W. Fowler, *Stages of Faith* (San Francisco: Harper & Row, 1981).

3. Wayne Rickerson, *Family Fun and Togetherness* (Wheaton, Ill.: Victor Books, 1979); *Christian Family Activities*, 3 vols. (Cincinnati: Standard Publishing, 1982). Also in the same series is one for single-parent families by Bobbie Reed. Walk Through the Bible Ministries, Inc. (P.O. Box 80587, Atlanta, GA 80587) has recently begun publication of a monthly family devotional guide, *Family Walk*, under the direction of Bruce Wilkinson.

4. Dolores Curran, *Traits of a Healthy Family* (Minneapolis: Winston Press, 1983) pp. 217-229.

7
Dealing Positively With Crisis

*T*he final quality that Stinnett and his associates found in strong families was the ability to deal with crises and major problems in a positive way. In even the darkest of situations, they saw hope and did not despair. Somehow, when difficult times came, they managed to pull together, when weaker families would have fragmented. This trait, like the others, does not rise in isolation, but is intricately interwoven with the other good qualities. Let's look into this fascinating area of family strength forged in adversity.

Definition of a Crisis
A crisis is an emotional response to a hazardous situation. It is a crossroads, a turning point, a transitional period. The Greek word from which we get our English word means "judgment or decision." Crisis is more than a routine upset. A true crisis occurs when people find themselves unable to solve a problem by their usual means. They have a feeling of helplessness and are unable to reason effectively and cope normally. A crisis is an emotional overload, the loss of something deemed essential to survival, usually emotional survival.

A crisis is a subjective state, caused by the personal meaning attributed to an event. So in one way, we can say that the crisis is not caused by the event itself, but by the person's reaction to that event. That reaction ties in heavily with the person's past experiences. You have probably seen various families who are struck by similar tragic events. Some of them grow closer and are stronger after working through the crisis, while others are torn apart. The difference, at least in part, is in the ways they have chosen to react to the situation. Their interpretation of what is happening is the key.

There are two broad categories of crisis. The first is *developmental*, those crises that predictably occur during transitional periods in the human life cycle. The first day of school (how many of you cried?), adolescence, leaving home, getting married, having children, mid-life occurrences, retirement—these all have their times of crisis in varying degrees. The second type is *accidental*, hazards of life that are less expected but, nevertheless, inevitable. Physical illness or injury, loss of employment, failure in business, and divorce are but a few examples. It's interesting to see where people categorize death—as developmental or accidental. I suppose that most of us would call it accidental. Nearly all the folks I have known who died did so "prematurely," no matter what their age.

Lloyd Ahlem, in his excellent book, *How to Cope with Conflict, Crisis and Change*, delineates four phases in the crisis sequence: impact, withdrawal-confusion, adjustment, reconstruction-reconciliation. He describes the attendant characteristics of each phase and concludes with a practical list of how to cope well in a crisis.[1]

It is helpful for all of us to understand the dynamics of crisis, both for ourselves and others. What we say and do for others during a crisis depends on where they are in the crisis stage. This type of insight has very practical value in a world of uncertainty and stress.

Family Survival Factors

Again I ask, "Why do some families make it through a crisis when others don't?" Are there components of strong families that can be identified and taught to other families? I believe there are some identifiable traits that can help all of us through those rough times in our families. Let's take a look at them.

• How the family crisis is viewed. We have already seen that how the crisis is interpreted is a major factor in reaction to the crisis. Families have a style of reacting to crisis, just as an individual does. In strong families, developmental crises are anticipated and characterized by preplanning. These families seem to accept periodic stresses as a necessary part of change in their lives.

Also important is how a family redefines the crisis after its initial stage. Often, after regaining their equilibrium, they will begin breaking the problem down into manageable parts. It may be necessary to adopt an active process of mental resignation or a conscious reduction of demands. Things which they cannot change, as a result of the crisis, they accept as inevitable. They will work on finding alternate ways of satisfying their needs.

The tendency of some families is to "catastrophize" in a crisis situation. That only intensifies the stress and delays the recovery process. If one crisis is not settled successfully, another awaits. Perhaps you know families who live from one crisis to the next. Healthy families, while obviously not enjoying crises, nevertheless look for the redeeming qualities that can come out of them. Thus, an extremely important factor in how families deal with upsetting events is their mind-set going into the crisis.

• Support systems. Dr. Hamilton McCubbin has done a significant amount of research on how families deal with stress. His conclusion is that families and individuals are profoundly affected by their network of social support.[2] He mentions three sources of support: neighborhoods, family and kin, and mutual support groups. I want to add a fourth for Christians—the church. That element will be discussed a little later. But here I want to make the point that families usually don't face crisis alone. They are helped or hindered by those around them. McCubbin says that a person or family can withstand even the most severe kind of crisis if the system of support around them is of sufficient quality.

We have seen also that the healthy family does not stay to itself but reaches out to others. Thus, strong ties of relationship are being continually developed. When the crisis comes, the support system is ready to rally around them.

This need for a strong network of friends compels me to remind all of us to be sensitive to new families who move into our neighborhoods, schools, and churches. Many of them have had to leave their support systems behind. Starting all over is not easy. It has taken our family about two years in each new location to really feel that we are part of a support network. Others may adjust more quickly, but they would probably be the exception. Family moves from one city to another are definitely crises. Let's keep a careful eye out for those who are needing to build a group of new friends for support. The church growth experts tell us that if there isn't significant progress in a church fellowship toward a new member's formation of a support group within a year, he will probably drop out.

• Values and meaning of life. A crisis, in addition to the immediate and visible effects, can cause an examination of values and meaning in life. "What does life mean?" "How can I make sense out of what is happening to me or my family?" "Why did God allow this to happen to us?" These deeper questions are usually raised in a family crisis by everyone involved.[3] A careful distinction needs to be made here. It is not the raising of questions that determines the outcome. Even the strongest Christians among us ask these questions. A number of God's servants in the Bible asked them too.

Because strong families know who they are and what they believe, they can weather the crisis, gathering strength from the stability that conviction gives. They may waver temporarily, but overall their period of adjustment is easier because of the anchors in their lives. They eventually bring some ultimate sense and meaning out of seeming nonsense.

• Religious grounding. You will recognize this factor as one of Stinnett's major characteristics of strong families. In this context I want to focus on the role of religious conviction in the family during a time of trial. Two passages of Scripture apply in a particular way to our present focus. The first is Romans 8:28. Paul says, "And we know that in all things God works for the good of those who love Him, who have been called according to His purpose." Notice that Paul does not say that whatever happens will be good. The promise is that *God will work through whatever happens* to bring about something redemptive for Christians who remain true to their calling. This verse in a special way captures the spirit of optimism that strong families exhibit, even in the darkest of circumstances.

The second passage is James 1:2-4. In his introductory remarks, James said:

> Consider it pure joy, my brothers, whenever you face trials of many kinds, because you know that the testing of your faith develops perseverance. Perseverance must finish its work so that you may be mature and complete, not lacking anything.

The redemptive and refining quality that is the product of Christian hardship stands out. Strong Christian families see crisis as an opportunity for growth. Here the growth exhibits itself in perseverance, hanging on, and stick-to-itiveness. When that quality is allowed to grow, the person—or the family—will be mature, full-grown, lacking nothing. Quite a promise, isn't it?

• Past successes. Here we are again faced with a basic principle of family interaction. Success breeds success and failure breeds failure. The more we act in a certain way, the more we are likely to act that way again. This principle is not a deterministic one, for these cycles of behavior can certainly be reversed. But it is a habit-forming one. Unless conscious effort is exerted, we will all follow the same rut, usually a negative one.

Dr. Jerry Lewis makes an interesting observation. He says, "Healthy families don't have to deal with chronic, internal stress that grows out of poor family relationships."[4] Therefore, they can save up their emotional energy for the major crises. The dysfunctional family drains itself on chronic, everyday problems. When a big one comes along, the straw-that-broke-the-camel's-back principle goes into effect. This wearing-down effect also causes tired families to catastrophize what may in effect not be a major crisis. But their reaction has made it seem so. Therefore, our past track record of how we have dealt with crises is at least some indicator of how we will deal with future ones if we continue our present course.

• Expression of feelings. All crisis involves the loss of something, usually something we see as essential to our emotional survival. Therefore, Dr. Jerry Lewis' statement about loss and the attendant feelings is extremely important.

> Perhaps the single most important family characteristic which influences the family's capacity to deal with loss is the ability to be open with feelings. The feelings of shock, anger, and profound sadness that follow the death of a loved one will be experienced by all. The question is, will they be felt only alone or will there be some sharing? Those families who can share openly such painful feelings encourage a sense of being

together which offers some easing of the painful wound. For those who do not have this type of openness, each family member's pain must be experienced alone, and this adds to the burden.[5]

• Flexibility and change. A key to all the adaptability factors is the family's ability to change and be flexible. I like to watch track meets. One of my favorite events is the pole vault. What if the vaulters used glass poles instead of fiberglass? You know that on the first attempt at a vault, the pole, if it was bent at all, would break because it was rigid and brittle. But the fiberglass pole bends, and the force of that flexibility is the very thing that propels the vaulter toward his goal. So it is in families. The key is flexibility—the ability to bend without breaking—and adaptability to change.

Change is inevitable. Change happens internally within the family and outside the family. I like the old Eastern proverb that says, "No man steps into the same river twice." The stream of time moves on. The healthy family makes constant adjustment to time and the inevitable changes it brings. The unhealthy family spends a lot of time trying to stop the river!

Crisis Can Produce Growth

All these survival factors that we see in strong families are interrelated. For purposes of discussion I have had to separate them. But now it's time to put them back together and say that where a high degree of one element is found, usually there are others as well.

Crisis can produce growth in families. Often in troubled times we learn to rely on one another more, and we begin to see qualities in people we had not seen before. One successful coping can lead to further successes. The biblical view that Christian growth takes place in an individual in its finest form in stressful situations is also true of family units.

A final comment on growth. I'm not sure growth actually takes place in the crisis itself, at least in the early stage. At the impact stage of a crisis, the only resources we have are the ones we bring into the crisis, the ones we have developed in more peaceful times. As an outgrowth of the crisis event, we may do some growing. But Christianity is not a Band-Aid religion. It can't be applied only when we hurt. It has to be lived on a daily basis. Therefore, the families that benefit most from crises are those that work on their relationships continually and not just when they are drawn together by a common adversity.

Footnotes

1. Lloyd Ahlem, *How to Cope with Conflict, Crisis, and Change* (Glendale, Calif.: Regal, 1978).

2. Hamilton McCubbin, "Broadening the Scope of Family Strengths: An Emphasis on Family Coping and Social Support," in Nick Stinnett, *et al.* (eds), *Family Strengths 3* (Lincoln, Neb.: University of Nebraska Press, 1981), pp. 177-194.

3. Howard Stone, *Crisis Counseling* (Philadelphia: Fortress Press, 1976), p. 23.

4. Jerry M. Lewis, *How's Your Family? A Guide to Identifying Your Family's Strengths and Weaknesses* (New York: Brunner/Mazel, 1979), p. 136.

5. Jerry M. Lewis, *How's Your Family?* p. 170.

8
Mixing the Ingredients

*W*ouldn't you like to have a family that consistently had all six characteristics I have just described? I would too. These outstanding characteristics can't possibly be in one family all the time. On the other hand, they are not impossible, pie-in-the-sky goals. What the researchers are telling us is that there are a lot of healthy families running around out there. These traits can be achieved on realistic levels. Of course, every family must seek its own level of competence. But the good news is that wherever your family is, it can improve.

These characteristics are so interwoven, it is difficult to have one without the others. From a Christian perspective, we should not be surprised at this. Many of the Christian virtues build on one another and are usually found together. I am reminded of Peter's admonition:

> For this very reason, make every effort to add to your faith goodness; and to goodness, knowledge; and to knowledge, self-control; and to self-control, perseverance; and to perseverance, godliness; and to godliness, brotherly kindness; and

to brotherly kindness, love. For if you possess these qualities in increasing measure, they will keep you from being ineffective and unproductive in your knowledge of our Lord Jesus Christ (2 Peter 1:5-8).

I promised you practicality, reality, and honesty in building strong families. Let me sum up Section 1 by offering some suggestions that will honor these criteria.

1. *Decide that you want a stronger family.* At the risk of sounding a bit trite, this is the place to begin. I talk to far too many families who would ultimately rather gripe about the rut they're in than take the effort to get out. Change, particularly into the unknown, is scary, and some people settle for miserable circumstances rather than launch out into a way they've never tried before.

If you have a faltering family, you may not be convinced that it can be any different. I say that it can, and the beginning point for you is to decide that you want this.

2. *Begin doing things that strong families do.* If you wait until the time is just right or until everybody feels like working on family strengths, you may never get started. One of the most powerful principles of learning is modeling and learning by example. If I read good solid research that says strong families have certain characteristics, and if I see these in good families I know, that's powerful. The conclusion is that as we imitate the model, we will become more like it. That's why Paul could say, in 1 Corinthians 11:1, "Follow my example, as I follow the example of Christ." The same thought is in Philippians 4:9 and 1 Peter 2:21. Do what strong families do and you will grow stronger.

3. *Keep reading books and articles that will help you.* A lot of good material is being written today on family strengths.

Family-oriented magazines, for the most part, are helpful in digesting good tips to increase your quality of life together—especially magazines with a Christian orientation.

A word of caution here. Beware of creating false expectations for your family. What will work in someone else's situation may not work in yours. Every family is a unique blend of personalities and needs. Find a comfortable level of growth and don't get too much in a hurry. Everyone in the family may not see the need for change that you do. While you can't change them, you can make a decision to incorporate these strengths to a greater degree in your own life. In the end, the change really does have to take place on a personal level. You can be the first to begin.

4. *Reach out to other families.* One thing we have seen is that the healthy family does not exist in isolation. It exists in community. I am not equating health with overinvolvement in activities that pull families in all directions. I am talking about the development of a meaningful support system outside the family that spans generations. For Christians, the church can be a source for much of this support network. The "burden bearing" Paul talks about in Galatians 6:2 is a necessary part of life for families. And that job cannot be done adequately within the confines of the family exclusively. Reaching out takes courage and initiative. But keep reaching out until you touch someone and make them a part of your life.

5. *Pray for God to help you.* We Christians are a funny lot. We profess to be in contact with the greatest power this universe has ever known—God Almighty. And yet, at times we forget to utilize that power. To paraphrase Psalm 127:1, unless the Lord builds your family stronger, you labor in vain. I believe that prayer is a change agent in the lives of Christians. Two passages of Scripture that are my favorites on prayer are full of comfort and promise:

Do not be anxious about anything, but in everything by prayer and petition, with thanksgiving, present your requests to God. And the peace of God, which transcends all understanding, will guard your hearts and your minds in Christ Jesus (Phil. 4:6-7).

Ask and it will be given to you; seek and you will find; knock and the door will be opened to you. For everyone who asks receives; he who seeks finds; and to him who knocks, the door will be opened (Matt. 7:7-8).

6. Keep on keeping on! Change takes a lot of time and effort. But the results of the effort are worth the price. I suppose the most common mistake newlyweds make is their gross underestimation of the amount of effort and time it takes to produce quality family relationships. When I got married, that certainly was true. Developing good relationships takes a lot of work and patience, and I don't know of any shortcuts. But I do know one thing—it is certainly worth the effort because it is hard to be happier than your family is. We grow together. You may lose a few battles along the way, but you *can* win the war.

7. Spread the good news about strong families to the church. Up to this point, I have emphasized how your family is able to combine all these essentials for enrichment into a workable plan for yourselves.

In the next section I want to focus on how you can help build strong families in your church and community. The emphasis will be on how to instill these qualities of strength into other families. If you know what makes healthy families, why not build these principles and their parallel biblical concepts into your programs of Christian education and outreach? It can be done, and here's how. . . .

Section 2

9
Will It Work in the Church?

A woman who has been married twenty-six years sobs uncontrollably as she relates how her husband has left her for another woman. An elderly man, having to care for his wife of over fifty years who has lost her mind and her health, grapples with guilt feelings over his weariness and frustration. A beautiful teenage girl says with little emotion, "I hate my mother." A young couple with a new baby is already contemplating divorce. A middle-aged husband, who has put his job before his wife and children for fifteen years, stares into open space as he struggles to make it alone. Single again, a young divorcee tries to figure out what went wrong.

These are people I talked with in my experience as director of the Family Life Center at the South National Church of Christ in Springfield, Missouri. Yet not all the hurting people live in Springfield. You know some of them; you may be one of them. You can find them in the church and outside the church. They are businessmen, teachers, workmen, homemakers, and clerks. Most have been to Sunday School; some have even taught. They are people, and where people are, God is. As Christians, we are the instruments of God's peace in this world. The church is to reflect the concern of God. My purpose is to show that God's Word affirms the efforts of churches and individual Christians who reach out and minister to families.

A definition of some key terms is in order for purposes of clarity. I am using the word *family* in its broadest context to mean people who are married and single, widowed and divorced, children and adults. In one sense, every person is a member of a family of some sort.

When I refer to *family ministry* or *family life program*, I find that some people think I am talking about a million dollar gymnasium which a church builds primarily for family recreational programs. While such facilities are nice to have, that is not what I mean. I am talking about developing a ministry or program, not a facility. In many cases, this does not involve great expense. A congregation of any size can develop some type of family ministry and still stay within its financial capacity.

When I speak of a family life ministry, I mean more than establishing a counseling center, although counseling may well play a part. My firm conviction is that the most effective answer to the problem of family disintegration is a preventive approach. It is the only reasonable way that the church can ever gain on this growing problem.

The preventive approach involves classes, seminars, workshops, retreats, films, and activities that are designed to strengthen family relationships. These offerings should be built around stress points in the life cycle of the family—preparation for marriage, arrival of first child, coping with adolescence, the empty nest, retirement, and death. Other factors that put pressure on the family are: moving, job demands, economic problems, job change, long illness, and the subtle pressures that our secular society puts on us.

People will listen and respond to Christians who offer

help in coping with the stresses and strains of their families, if they see their needs being met. In fact, they may be more willing to listen to the Lord and His way during stress than at any other time of their lives. Family problems sap an enormous amount of time and energy, and some of this energy drain could be avoided by a well-planned program of prevention designed to equip people with the necessary coping skills.

I am talking about families on two levels. One level deals with the care and enrichment of Christian families in a congregation. The other level deals with families in the community. The two levels of ministry are complementary and should be pursued together.

Although the word *family* is used in the Old Testament some 250 times, the occurrence of the word in any English translation of the New Testament is rare. Yet, I know of hardly any other subject that appears more frequently in its various manifestations and implications than the concept of family relationships. At virtually any opening of your New Testament you will find some reference to how people are to get along with one another. My method of biblical investigation is to search for broad principles which underlie the central message of the Bible, rather than to use the proof-text method.

I am interested in doing more than simply justifying a biblical basis for family life ministries. My greater purpose is to show the desirability and even necessity of meeting family needs, if the church is to be what Christ wants it to be. Consider six reasons why I believe God is concerned about family life and why His church should be.

God's Care for Families

• God chose the analogy of the family to convey the revelation of Himself to mankind. Of all the analogies known to man, God chose the concept of *father* in its purest and finest sense to convey His relationship to mankind. Jesus Christ, the most precious gift of heaven, is described as the only begotten Son of God. The church is pictured by Paul as the bride of Christ. We are brothers and sisters, another family analogy. The institution of marriage was the first interpersonal relationship established by God. We can then conclude that God in all His wisdom believed that people could best understand His nature and His relationship to His creation through family terms.

• Jesus was concerned about family relationships and about meeting human needs. To the demon-possessed man, in Mark 5:19, Jesus said, "Go home to your family and tell them how much the Lord has done for you, and how He has had mercy on you." To the widow of Nain, in Luke 7, Jesus said, "Don't cry." Yet Luke records that Jesus' heart went out to her at the death of her only son. "God has come to help His people," the crowd shouted. And so He had. The list could go on and on—Jesus healing Peter's mother-in-law, helping lepers rejoin their families, healing sick children, restoring sight to the blind and hearing to the deaf—all the people were members of families that experienced great anxiety and loss in a crisis.

We need to take a close look at the real message of the judgment scene preview of Matthew 25. In each case of the redeemed responding to hunger, thirst, homelessness, nakedness, treatment of illness or visitation, a human need was met. Who are "the least of these brothers" of the Lord's, if they are not the people with whom we come into contact every day? He's not talking about people we never meet. He's talking about meeting the needs of people we see every day. What about the people *you* see every day? Do they have any family needs? Do they need to learn more effective ways of relating to their spouses or children or parents or in-laws? Are most of their families hurting and in trouble? I think the answer is obvious. Why should we limit the interpretation of meeting needs to physical manifestations only? Surely the emotional and psychological and spiritual needs are equally as important, if not more so.

• The stability of the church depends on the stability of families. I believe the Bible teaches that the family is the laboratory for Christianity. If it doesn't work at home, where does it work? What would happen in our families if each one of us here resolved to use Ephesians 4:29-32 as a model for our family relations?

> Do not let any unwholesome talk come out of your mouths, but only what is helpful for building others up according to their needs, that it may benefit those who listen. And do not grieve the Holy Spirit of God, with whom you were sealed for the day of redemption. Get rid of all bitterness, rage and anger, brawling and slander, along with every form of malice. Be kind and compassionate to one another, forgiving each other, just as in Christ God forgave you.

These admonitions of Paul are not designed just to tell us how to treat one another down at the church building. It's a real shame that we sometimes treat total strangers with more courtesy and respect than we do those of our own families.

Notice Paul's admonition to Timothy about the characteristics of a spiritual leader of the church: "He must manage his own family well and see that his children obey him with proper respect" (1 Tim. 3:4). Then Paul added a parenthetical question that revealed his intense concern about this important quality: "If anyone does not know how to manage his own family, how can he take care of God's church?" The home is the laboratory for Christian living. There is a decided emphasis in the New Testament on the development of family life. A church with strong families will be a strong church.

• A family ministry is an effective means of evangelism.

Christians are called upon to be light and salt and leaven in a chaotic world. We can decide to continue to talk to ourselves and spend money on ourselves, or we can with renewed commitment take the challenge of Jesus to make a difference in the lives of people in the world. A ministry to families is one good way to be involved as salt and leaven and light in the community. Over half the 1,100 people who had contact with our Family Life Center at the South National Church in 1980 were not members of that congregation. Many had no religious affiliation. Some of these people are now Christians; others are seeking and learning about Jesus. All these people sought *us* out; we did not have to search for them.

I was visiting recently with a missionary to Brazil. He told me that when they sponsor a series of meetings on the family, they will have about four times the number of visitors they would normally have for a traditional revival service. All over the world people are concerned about their families. Surely the Lord's people must feel compelled to bring the peace of Christ into these searching families.

The church growth experts say that by far the most effective way to evangelize is through family relationships. That's why what I am talking about is not an optional fringe program that we might want to pursue as a church. Family ministry in its manifold forms lies at the heart of what it means to be Christ's church.

Perhaps a word of warning would be in order. A meaningful program of family ministry may be hazardous to your status quo. As Jesus said, when you cast your net you will get all kinds of fish (Matt. 13). I am thinking of a man I worked with who had five wives. But as I recall, Jesus ran into a similar situation with a Samaritan woman. On that occasion He talked to her about living water and true worship and being His disciple (John 4). It would do us all well to remember that conversation when we face similar situations.

• The Bible teaches that man is a basic unit and cannot be compartmentalized. The Hebrew concept of the essential unity of man—from which the New Testament view of man is derived—forbids us to minister to spiritual needs alone and exclude other needs that interrelate. We are all aware of the close connection between one's physical problems and his emotional condition. The Bible's wholistic view of man should remind us that when family problems hit, they quite often cause spiritual problems within the family and, at times, even physical ailments.

The church's response to this wholistic view of man should be a ministry to families that will take into account not just their spiritual condition, but their emotional and physical and social condition as well. Family members profoundly affect one another. Therefore, when one member is having problems of any kind, it will affect all the members to some degree.

• The two main functions of a New Testament church are evangelism and edification. A family ministry blends these beautifully.

What can be more edifying to the body and glorifying to God than for families to learn how to enrich the quality of their lives together? Another aspect of edification is the widespread use of Christian volunteers to work in the family ministry programs. They are able to exercise a variety of spiritual gifts as they teach and counsel and encourage fellow Christians and community people.

The evangelism possibilities are tremendous, as previously mentioned. People are responsive to the claims of the Gospel after they have seen that Christian people genuinely care about their individual and family problems. In my experience in family life ministry, I have seen a high degree of community acceptance and encouragement. People appreciate a church that is willing to show its faith by its works in a way that will benefit family life. The family enrichment emphasis is one of low controversy and high interest, thus enabling us to break down some religious prejudice. I think of the religion editor of a local newspaper who, on receiving news of the beginning of our family ministry, bluntly remarked to me, "Finally, a church is putting its money where its mouth is!"

A Challenge to the Church

Contemporary marriage and family experts are reminding us that in previous generations the important factors holding families together were largely external and brought on by economic necessity. But today marriages can no longer be held together by external coercion. People are demanding more than that. What *will* hold them together is *internal cohesion*, based on improved interpersonal relationships, and that can be taught. The Bible has plenty to say on that subject.

What I am calling for is a renewed emphasis in the church on training people in interpersonal relationships. The vast majority of people who get married and have families have received practically no training for the day-to-day relationships of husband and wife, parent and child—their communication with each other, their clashing wills, their needs for fulfillment and emotional security. Do you think that God's Word gives some direction along these lines? Do you think that the church has anything to offer hurting families in our day? Do you think there's a biblical basis for a family life ministry?

How do we go about it? The answer is a complex one. But just a word about *how* people learn. Providing information is not enough to bring about behavioral and relational change. Dr. David Mace points out that change requires two further processes; there must be *insight*, which interprets information to enable us to explain and understand our own functioning, and *action*, which is necessary before insight can be put to use. He says that marriage counseling is not the answer. While it is necessary and helpful, it is *remedial* and not *preventive*. For Dr. Mace, the two brightest spots in an otherwise troubled contemporary family picture are an increasing awareness of the importance of the subject and the marriage enrichment movement.[1]

It is Dr. Mace's firm conviction, and mine, that the church is in an ideal position to lead out and make a difference in the quality of family life in our world. Richard Wilke estimated in 1974 that up to 80 percent of those with marriage and family problems go first to see a minister.[2] While that percentage may be a little high for a decade later, there is no doubt that the percentage is still well over 50 percent. The opportunities are great, but the task is formidable. We do not react with indifference when our economy goes into decline, when our environment becomes polluted, when epidemics or natural disasters strike. Neither can we afford to act with indifference when our family life is in danger. What will it profit us to gain the whole world and lose our families?

If you detect a note of urgency in this message, it is because there is. I believe with all my heart that God has ordained the family to love each other and serve each other and provide comfort and strength and encouragement to one another. I believe that the biblical basis for a family ministry lies in the fact that God loves people, that people are part of families, and that He cares very much how they treat one another. I believe that if we are to do the work of God on this earth, we are going to have to focus our attention on family matters, not because it is the current fad, but because it is God's will. With God's help and our participation, we will make a difference. Together, we can build strong families!

Now, let's get to the business at hand and see how this bold dream can become a reality in your church.

Footnotes

1. David Mace, "Marriage in Transition: Implications for Social Policy," *Pastoral Psychology*, 1977, 25, pp. 236-247.
2. Richard Wilke, *The Pastor and Group Marriage Counseling* (Nashville: Abingdon, 1974), p. 18.

10
Foundations of Family Ministry

I hope I have convinced you that something *can* and *should* be done in your church about development of a family ministry. Now, what's the next step? Remember that family ministry is not something you *add* to your regular church program. It must be integrated throughout all that the church does, and this will mean that you expand and improve on the existing programs.

In this section, we're going to go back and reinforce some foundations of family ministry so that we will be able to build an increasing quality and quantity of services that reach out to families. It's somewhat like adding floors to an existing building. The first thing the contractor does is to shore up the existing foundation so that the building will withstand the weight and the stress that the addition will bring. To use Jesus' terms in Luke 6:48, we want to be sure that we lay our foundation on rock, not on sand.

The temptation is to start programs and activities in random fashion as they flow naturally out of our enthusiasm and our concerns for families. Yet this directionless, shortsighted foundation will last only temporarily.

All ministries are built on a set of assumptions. Everything the church does has theological and procedural assumptions that underlie it. The difference between the houses that stand and those that fall lies in the awareness and assessment of the basic assumptions on which they were built. The careful builder will spend a lot of time in planning and becoming aware of the far-reaching implications of what he is about to do. Then, when the floods of reality strike the house, it will stand.

The appearance of those parabolic houses on the rock and on the sand may well have been identical. The difference was in the foundations. Let's spend a little time looking at some foundations of family ministry that will insure stability and give direction, purpose, and cohesiveness.

Family Ministry Should be Primarily Preventive

As I talk with church leaders throughout the country, one of the most poignant questions they ask is, "What can we do to stem the tide of family disintegration in our churches?" It's a critical question. Even the most casual observer can see that the answer is not simply to train more counselors. The adage, "It makes a lot more sense to build a fence around the top of the cliff than it does to put an ambulance at the bottom," is graphically true in family ministry.

Family difficulties are so pervasive that it is impossible for ministers and mental health professionals to see all the troubled families. To assume that a significant number of troubled families will ever seek out professional help is unrealistic. Besides, most families do not stand in need of that advanced a level of help. The strategy that makes the most sense is to equip families with the necessary coping skills so that they may deal with issues effectively *before* full-blown crises develop.

At the heart of preventive fence-building is the transmission of effective problem-solving techniques and conflict-resolution skills that will serve to defuse negative family communication. Big marital and family problems have small beginnings. The Bible has a lot to say about how we are to get along with one another. An effective family ministry will reflect positive teaching toward focusing on problems and conflicts while they are still manageable.

An ounce of prevention is worth about a ton of cure! While we must always be sensitive to those for whom prevention is too late, our aim in family ministry should decidedly be to equip and build up in a preventive mode. If Humpty Dumpty had never fallen off that wall, "all the king's horses and all the king's men" would have had a much easier time. We must keep in clear focus our primary goal—to keep families and marriages together by providing opportunities for growth and strength and wellness. Family ministry is a lot more than a counseling service.

Emphasis Should be on Building Family Strengths

Until recently, the disciplines of psychology, psychiatry, marriage and family therapy, and family studies have focused on what was wrong with individuals and families. Even today, much of what we read is based on pathology—the sickness, the dysfunction—rather than the wellness model. Mental health definitions are often based on the absence of certain pathologies. It's not a very optimistic approach.

But fortunately, the tide is turning. More and more emphasis is being given to the positive aspects of individual and family wellness. Strong families are now being studied, and traits are being isolated that can be taught. The first section of this book deals with some of the characteristics found in strong families.

The study of positive family models has provided a much needed balance. The Bible speaks of "building one another up," teaching, encouraging, and dwelling on positive things. That's what I need to inspire me. I'd much rather talk with a family that is loving and well and making a go of it than one that is falling apart. Positive models are far more inspiring than negative ones in creating a healthy family atmosphere.

Now that we know what makes strong families, what is the practical application in the life of the church? The present foundational principle simply says: whatever is planned for families to do and to be in your church must reflect a positive, edifying, inspiring model of Christian family life, rather than a negative, pathological one.

Programs Should be Developed with an Awareness of the Transition and Crisis Points in the Family Life Cycle

In the past several years, increased attention has been given to a study of the human life span from a developmental perspective. Building on the pioneering work of VanGennep, Freud, Jung, and Erikson, social scientists have been particularly interested in the development of the adult life cycle. They saw that adults continue to go through stages of development, just as children do. Now, thanks to the work of people like Daniel Levinson and others, major contributions have been made to the understanding of adult growth and change.[1]

Jim and Sally Conway were among the first evangelicals to call attention to adult developmental stages, with their work on men in mid-life crisis.[2] Since their work in the late 1970s and early 1980s, others have followed.

In 1977, Claud Guldner proposed a "warranty model for human relationships" in which he saw marriage and family living as a series of loops in an ongoing developmental lifeline. These loops consist of two parts: the pre-level or preparation period and the actual experience. Guldner's point is that emphasis should be placed on both the "pre" period and the "neo" or early period in order to maximize the successful management of the transition phases of human living. He centers his approach around the traditional adult family transition points of pre-marriage, early marriage, parenting, adolescent parenting, empty nest, retirement, and death of spouse.[3]

An effective family ministry must incorporate the recent emphases among developmentalists. If the preventive approach is taken seriously, we need programs in our churches that will equip adults to cope successfully with the transition points in adult growth. Whether they are prepared will often determine if an event is a transition or a crisis point.

And yet, as Guldner points out, preparation for a transition is not enough. One cannot really appreciate a life phase until one is living in it. Therefore, family life programs need to reflect an awareness of preparation for people's life transitions, plus organization and direction of that experience in its early stages. Perhaps the best example of the need to follow through beyond the preparation stage is evidenced in premarital work. Studies now show conclusively that maximum benefit is gained only if there is follow-through in the first year of marriage.

The Development of a Strong Social Support System Needs to be Emphasized

It is generally agreed among family specialists that there is a qualitative difference in the relationship of the basic or nuclear family unit to its extended family today, as compared to preindustrial times. The decline of extended family contacts may be a major factor in the loneliness and isolation within many Christian homes. On several occasions in metropolitan area churches, I have asked those people who had no immediate relatives within a twenty-five-mile radius of where they lived to raise their hands. Usually about half the congregation raised their hands. We must therefore realize that most churches are composed of a significant number of people who are cut off from their kin.

As a result of the isolation from extended family and the social isolation from the surrounding community, the nuclear family turns inward to each other for mutual help and support. These increased intimate relationships now have to carry a heavier load than in past generations. No one is present to help dilute family tensions. Therefore, each friction point has within it the elements of a full-blown crisis. Added to this internal family emotional overload is the contemporary quest for intimacy. If the price for family intimacy is the abandonment of meaningful social contacts outside the home, the cost is too great.

Churches that are serious about effective family ministry need to concentrate on reconnecting the isolated family and the community. The church ministers to people who are separated from one another and who are overloaded in their internal family support systems. Attention to the internal welfare of family units is not enough. We must also be aware that the family may be suffering because it is being cut off from other people.

Individuals have a desperate need for community life as well as a rewarding family life. We must increase our attention to providing community life and meaningful fellowship for our Christian families. Isn't that part of what it means to be the family of God?

Family Ministry Should be Contemporary and Realistic

Modern families are profoundly influenced by industrialization and technology. They live in a fast-paced world and they struggle for creative answers to their problems. The task of the church is to make ancient biblical truths relevant to contemporary family circumstances. We have a growing number of family specialists, both within the Christian context and beyond, who are making significant contributions in assisting contemporary families.

Being contemporary requires a realistic view. A realistic family ministry must deal with frustration, pain, disappointment and conflict, as well as the joys that come from living together as a family. The struggles are complicated, and no easy solutions are on the horizon. Facing these matters realistically is a beginning.

Family Ministry Must Serve a Variety of Family Types

Traditionally, the word *family*, when used within the church context, meant a husband, his one and only wife, and their children—*the nuclear family*. The wife usually was not gainfully employed outside the home. Today the key word to describe the American family is *change*. The nuclear family as described above accounts for less than one-third of the American population, even with counting the dual career families. And the percentage is dropping steadily. Single people and single-parent families, as well as stepfamilies, are on the rise.

In the past, the reaction of evangelical churches to the changing family structure has generally been neglect, at best, or outright rejection, at worst. In recent years, however, the trend has been to recognize as legitimate a variety of family forms: single; married, with children; married, without children; and the formerly married, with children and without. These forms can be recognized, while at the same time holding to a strong theological stance of pro-marriage and anti-divorce. The two positions are not necessarily contradictory.

Charles Sell suggests four ways church programming and planning can take into account the many family forms and minister to all families.

• Embrace all forms of the family in communicating and structuring. The way the church talks about families needs to be redefined to include everyone. For instance, activities involving fathers and their children may cause pain to the single parent mother and her children who are excluded. Family retreats can and should be designed to include a variety of family types (even singles), so that no one feels left out.

• Build the church as a family. While technically the church is not an extended family, it may well function as one. The effects of separation and isolation from kin can be reduced when church members feel part of a church family. This effect can be accomplished through intergenerational and interfamily groups.

• Create special groups to meet special needs. People feel the need to relate to those who are facing similar circumstances. Singles, single parents, those widowed, and older people will especially benefit from the mutual support. A word of caution here—most people who fall into these categories do not like to be segregated from the rest of the church all the time. They like the benefit of general church fellowship, as well as time with those of similar circumstances.

• Deal with family issues and crises. Many modern family changes come about as the result of a crisis within the family. People who have been through traumatic crises need special attention, such as those who are divorced, separated, and widowed. Other situations provide a mixture of positive and negative pressures on family members; for example, those who are newly married, parents, stepfamilies, and retired people.

Attention must be given to where modern families are, as well as to where they ought to be. Family ministry programs that do not take these conditions into account will be largely ineffective.

Family Ministry Should be Home-Centered as Well as Church-Centered
Protestant churches have patterned themselves primarily

after the institutional, task-centered approach that dominates the business world, rather than establishing a family dynamic within the fellowship. Particularly has this been true among evangelical churches. The result has been relationships that tend to be superficial, with little training in familylike relationships. In fact, the development of interpersonal relationships, as one would find in a family context, is perceived as hindering the church's fulfillment of its corporate task. The time that the institutional church requires competes with family time and often hinders family relationships. Contemporary church leaders we have held up as examples often tend to be task-oriented, production-conscious people who have little time for their own families. As we see the results of this misguided zeal on Christian family life, we need to take a second look at our priorities.

The institutional church finds itself in an ironic situation. On the one hand, the church is to stand for and promote good family relationships. On the other hand, it may be fostering the opposite in its practical effects. If we believe that the church is more like a family than anything else, that one concept will have profound effects on the modern "business" model some of our churches have unwisely adopted.

Another troublesome question is whether the church should take the place of the family in the training of children, or whether its role is to equip parents to train their own children. The response of the institutional church leaders is that they are having to do the job by default, because the parents are not. Also, through evangelistic efforts, many churches see an increasing number of children who do not have Christian parents or who have only one parent who is a Christian. Therefore, it falls on the institutional church to be the primary trainer of these children.

With a realization of the complexity of the problem and

a sensitivity to the roles of both home and church, I firmly believe that the home should take an increasing responsibility in the nurturing of children in Christian families. And the church should encourage the return to the biblical model that is as old as Moses' admonition to God's people, in Deuteronomy 6:4-9. My parental responsibility for the spiritual development of my children cannot be assumed by the church as a whole. The church can and should act as a *supplement* to my efforts, but not as a substitute.

Church life is more distinct from family life than it should be. The order should be that the church life is patterned after the home life, rather than the reverse. The church and the home can enter into a mutually beneficial relationship, whereby both can be strengthened. The possibility that the modern family will be "underresponsible" and that the church will be "overresponsible" is a real one. In its requests for participation of people in its varied ministries, the church will need to be cautious that these demands not be counterproductive to the welfare of its greatest human resources—people in families.

Family Ministry Needs to be Experienced as well as Taught

In our society, the normal way to obtain an education is through the assimilation of facts. In many areas of life, information is all that is needed. Providing information, however, is not of itself a significant means of bringing about behavioral or relational change. Particularly is this true when it is applied to marriage and family education. In churches where biblical authority is strongly embraced, there is the tendency to view teachings on family life as simply getting the information out to the people—"What do you mean, we still have the problem? We had a lesson on that last month!" David Mace reveals the complexity and futility of the problem when he points out,

The barrier to using information to achieve *relational* change is even more formidable, because it is necessary for *two* persons, acting together, to move through insight to joint action. This being so, I would hypothesize that practically all of the information about marriage that is propagated has no effect whatsoever on the lives of those who are the recipients of it.[4]

Family Ministry Should Be Expanded to Include Offerings to the Community

The usual boundaries for development of a family life ministry are within the context of the church fellowship. A preferable model assumes a dual approach to family ministry, with one emphasis on church families and the other on families in the community at large. The family enrichment emphasis is one of low controversy and high interest. Everyone is interested in some way in bringing about better family and interpersonal relationships. If they see their needs being met, people will listen and respond to Christians who offer help in coping with the stresses and strains of their families.

The courses and other services designed particularly for community appeal generally center around times of crisis and transition in the family life cycle. The weeknight and weekend offerings could include preparation for marriage, prenatal, parenting, marriage enrichment, divorce adjustment, etc. A word of warning—if these offerings to the community by the church become simply a front for high-pressure evangelism, community people will not support them. Dealing with the spiritual dimensions of life is a legitimate area of concern for the church, and one in which it should be involved. It is the *manner* in which these are presented that is the issue. People in the community should be able to hear the subjects presented from a Christian perspective without feeling pressured to conform to a particular set of sectarian beliefs. Spiritual matters should be presented to them as a choice rather than a mandate. The church can and should present its family material from a Christian perspective without being offensive to people who do not share their belief system.

Christians are called upon to be light and salt and leaven in a chaotic world and to do good to all people. Some churches have a decision to make—will they talk to themselves, or will they take the challenge of Jesus to make a difference in the lives of people? An effective community outreach program to families is one good way to make faith come alive through action. The combined attention to church families and to community families is effective. Each is made richer by involvement with the other.

Family Ministry Needs to Operate from a Theological Foundation

Theology should be an integral part of all that the church is and does. It is not my purpose to present in detail a theological base for the church's involvement in a family ministry program. However, its importance cannot be over-estimated. The theological assumptions underlying the family emphasis will significantly determine the content and direction of the ministries.

Every church must work out its own practical theology. The extent of the development in this section will be to delineate some areas of concern that need to be addressed. Before a family ministry program is launched, the church involved should deal with the following biblical issues:
- the nature, basis, and permanence of marriage
- the theology of divorce and remarriage
- determination of legitimate lifestyles
- nature and purpose of the family
- the theology of parenting
- the relationship between the family and the church
- the theology of sin, repentance, forgiveness, grace, and mercy as it relates to marriage and family matters

• biblical authority as applied to these contemporary situations of marriage and family.

An effective family ministry will surface a multitude of problems that have theological implications. Wise church leaders will anticipate as many as possible and seek to obtain some type of workable consensus beforehand.

Family Ministry Needs to be Integrated into Every Other Aspect of Church Life

The purpose of this section is to focus on the interrelatedness of the program with other existing functions of the church. Family ministry is far more than adding classes, seminars, and activities to an already crowded church schedule. It is more than hiring additional church staff. Churches that rely too much on added activities may produce the paradoxical effect of putting additional strain on families, rather than building them up. Family ministry activities, therefore, need to be integrated into the total life of the church.

• One way the integration can take place is for the family programs to be developed *within* existing ministries. Two areas particularly lend themselves to this integration. The educational ministry can offer marriage and family classes that become a part of the regular curriculum. Special seminars and workshops can also be planned. The youth ministry can plan intergenerational family activities such as parent-teen retreats, family campouts, family nights—any activity that involves the children and their parents. One encouraging trend among evangelical churches is to see youth ministers moving more toward ministry to entire families rather than to the children alone. Other ministries, such as benevolence, evangelism, and university student programs, can also incorporate an increased family awareness in their outlook and activities.

• A second and more important form of integration of

family ministry and the overall church involvement is the creation of a desire for a familylike atmosphere to permeate the church's being and purpose. This attitude reaches to the style of leadership as well as to the particular offerings. As we have already seen, churches in America tend to take on an institutional, board-of-directors form of leadership that is borrowed from the culture, not taken from the Bible. The isolation and loneliness of church members demand that church leaders provide a kind of family atmosphere within the fellowship that will meet these interpersonal needs. Charles Sell sees the creation of a family-church atmosphere as the most crucial task of the church today.[5] The church will only be as strong as its individual families are, whether they are nuclear, or whether they are "synthetic," as they find their place of acceptance within the larger church family.

The integration of families and individuals with one another will help counter the secular idea that the happy family is one that focuses inward on its own needs and desires. In an effort to instill individuality and self-respect in children, Christian families have a further obligation toward meeting the needs of others. The need for this emphasis led Tom Sine to ask, "Are we simply trying to preserve the family as it is—a family for itself; or are we attempting to transform it into what it needs to become—a family for others?"[6] While a proper balance is needed, the current tendency for families—Christians included—is to turn inward more than to reach out to others.

Footnotes

1. Daniel J. Levinson, et al., *The Seasons of a Man's Life* (New York: Alfred A. Knopf, 1978).
2. Jim Conway, *Men in Mid-Life Crisis* (Elgin, Ill.: Cook Publish-

ing, 1978); Sally Conway, *You and Your Husband's Mid-Life Crisis* (Elgin, Ill.: Cook Publishing, 1980); Jim and Sally Conway, *Women in Mid-life Crisis* (Wheaton, Ill.: Tyndale House, 1983).

3. Claud Guldner, "Marriage Preparation and Marriage Enrichment: The Preventive Approach," *Pastoral Psychology*, 1977, 25, pp. 248-259.

4. David Mace, "Marriage in Transition: Implications for Social Policy," *Pastoral Psychology*, 1977, 25, pp. 236-247.

5. Charles M. Sell, *Family Ministry: Family Life Through the Church* (Grand Rapids: Zondervan) pp. 74-85.

6. Tom Sine, "Becoming a Family for Others," *Family Life Today*, 1982, 8(6), pp. 8-10, 33.

11
Programs of
Family Ministry

*Y*our church can do something to enrich Christian family
life! No matter how small, there are several ideas that
can be implemented, many of them virtually cost-free. The
largest church I consulted about family ministry had several
thousand members. The smallest church had twelve members. Both are now engaged in meaningful ministries to
families. My hope is that this chapter will draw from you a
wealth of creative ideas to initiate in your own congregation. All of my suggestions will not be workable in every
situation. You may think of others that are better than mine.
Great! Give your creativity and imagination a real workout,
as you consider what would succeed best for you.

Education and Prevention
At the heart of the ministry to families is the prevention-
through-education theme. As stated in the previous chapter,
the objective is to equip people with the skills necessary to
help them negotiate their way through current and anticipated problems. Most people can solve their own problems
when they are given solid, practical instruction. But remember, the best way to learn is experientially—by doing.

Some of these offerings will adapt well to the Sunday or midweek time frame and objectives of a local church. Others may more appropriately be offered on a weekend format. Content, convenience, and identification of the target groups can determine your choice. Also length of time and concentration of courses will vary. The concentrated time frame, such as a weekend, is excellent for a renewal technique, where people focus intently on an issue in their family and make resolve to change positively. The once-a-week meetings have the advantage of lag time for absorption of the material and practical experimentation. Both approaches also have their disadvantages. The overall goals will determine the format and timetable.

• Preparation for marriage. Courses designed to prepare young people for marriage can be presented to various developmental levels. Actually, preparation for marriage begins in the cradle. In the early years of a child's life the learning process of mate selection begins to take place, whether or not there is guided instruction. Perhaps the most effective preparation for marriage could be developed during the preteen and early teen years before the active process of mate selection begins. The traditional preparation-for-marriage course is designed primarily for couples intending to marry or seriously considering marriage.

The basic goals are the same at all developmental levels, with appropriate adaptation to the age and circumstance. They are: proper mate selection, realistic expectations, adequate preparation, correct information, and development of healthy communication patterns. Since these five goals are essential for couples intending to marry, let's look at that level of marriage preparation in particular.

The classes for engaged couples should be offered by the family ministry on a periodic basis. Once in the spring and once in the fall may suffice to catch a majority of the couples. The course can be offered on a weeknight, thus increasing the possibility of couples coming from the community. For instance, it could be held every Monday evening in October and April from seven to ten. The three-hour periods give opportunity to build group rapport and couple interaction. The intervening days between classes allow for homework assignments to be done.

Two other formats can be used in addition to the class structure. A weekend retreat setting for engaged couples can be used effectively. Also, small group meetings, condensed in a weekend or extended to weekly meetings for a month or so, are helpful. Couples with strong marriages can lead these groups and serve as excellent role models.

The class setting or group discussion does not eliminate completely the need for premarital counseling.

It does, however, reduce the time needed in counseling and may bring to light problem areas that need particular attention. An increasing number of ministers are refusing to perform the marriage ceremony unless a couple has been through a premarital course and/or has had some counseling. Offering the course two or three times a year does save time for the minister, as well as focusing the church on the importance of marriage.

A number of testing and teaching resources are now available for use in preparation for marriage. The *Taylor-Johnson Temperament Analysis* is an excellent test for temperament compatability.[1] David Olson's new *Prepare* material holds great promise for assisting the minister in premarital counseling.[2] The *Marriage Expectation Inventory for Engaged Couples* is effective in uncovering each person's expectations regarding marriage and family issues.[3] The *Sex Knowledge Inventory* tests a person's comprehension of anatomy, physiology, and contraception.[4] An excellent workbook for the couples to use is Wright and Roberts' *Before You Say "I Do."*[5] The twelve sections deal with the major aspects of marriage, interweaving biblical teachings. The book has an ample supply of exercises that foster mutual discovery. Helpful for the course instructor and marriage counselor is Wright's *Premarital Counseling.*[6]

If a church is serious about prevention of marriage and family disruption, preparation for marriage should be of top priority. David Mace encourages going beyond the introduction to marriage to the newlywed stage. Since some problems will not surface until after the marriage, and since the first year is one of the most critical times of the marriage, some follow-through measures need to be developed. The church may choose to have an on-going group that meets once a month or may develop a weekly class through the existing curriculum. This type of effort to follow through will pay dividends in terms of marriages that begin on a solid footing and are likely to stay that way. Mace reminds us that we have a lot to learn about how to prepare two people for marriage. If you are serious about working with engaged couples or newlyweds, you need to read what this great leader in the field of marriage has to say. I heard him say recently (with tongue in cheek, no doubt) that everything he knew about marriage enrichment was in his book, *Close Companions.*[7]

• Marriage enrichment. There are many marriage enrichment formats currently in use. One of the most popular is the Marriage Encounter movement. Of Catholic origin, the movement is now under the sponsorship of several religious and secular groups. Also under the general banner of marriage enrichment, other creative programs have been launched. Most of these seek to increase intimacy, deepen mutual and self-understanding, and fit biblical goals of marriage and interpersonal relationships into the couple's lives.

The scheduling can be as varied as the content. One popular approach is the weekend retreat setting, usually at a motel. The advantages are a lack of outside detractions and an intense focus on the relationship. Dr. David Seamands, senior pastor of the United Methodist Church of Wilmore, Kentucky, has accomplished the same effect by having the seminar at the church building and placing strict requirements on the couple to farm out their children and be together alone throughout the weekend. Other schedules call for the class times to be on regular Sunday or midweek gathering times for the church, with assignments given between sessions.

Whatever the mode of marriage enrichment, the following factors should be considered when developing a program:

—It should be primarily affective, experiential education and should be billed as enrichment rather than therapy.

—Couples who are in serious marital trouble will likely not benefit from the experience. Their unresolved problems are so fragile that the "enrichment" experience may serve to draw matters to a crisis point rather than resolve them.

—Marriage enrichment should be voluntary. Some couples or individuals will feel uncomfortable in this setting and will see it as a threat.

—Guard against an exclusivistic attitude on the part o those who have been to a marriage enrichment experience of some kind. Couples who have not participated shoulc not be made to feel inferior.

—Long-range follow-up is desirable. Whether a weekenc experience or a course of several months' duration, the idea is to arrange a periodic follow-up on a sustained basis. Per haps monthly discussion groups could be organized. Th effects will be longer lasting if the principles are reinforce periodically.

—It is difficult to bring about significant change in a larg group setting. Couples have a tendency to get deeply ir grained in habits of interaction and unconsciously try t keep things the way they are. Change must take place o an individual basis, with growth in attitudes, values, em(tions, and spiritual perspectives. The efforts of marriaş enrichment programs are valid and needed, but realistic expectations and a precise assessment of human change agents must be a central part of those efforts.[8]

• Parent training (single and dual). Parenting programs abound in this country. The diversity has produced some confusion for church leaders. The result has been that many of them have devised their own programs, drawing from a variety of approaches, most heavily from James Dobson and Bruce Narramore. Of all the family enrichment programs, Christian parenting is the one most likely to already be in the curriculum of churches. The advantage of weeknight offerings is that parents from the community are able to participate. Schools and other public agencies are usually supportive if they are convinced of the quality of the course.

One approach is to break the parenting offerings into three separate areas. The first focuses on parenting the child from birth to age six. The second covers parenting of children in grades one through six. The third is for parents of adolescents. Each session could be two to four meetings. The advantage of this arrangement is that special attention can be given to each age category. The disadvantage is that parents may have children in more than one category. For the sake of time, I have increasingly gone to one-night sessions lasting for three hours. This ties up less time (mine and theirs) and eliminates the inevitable fallout on subsequent sessions.

Single parents, while having many of the same problems as dual parents, nevertheless, have problems that relate directly to their singleness. Separate courses could be offered. However, a more practical solution might be for single parents to form their own discussion group within the general parenting course or else form a mutual support group as an outgrowth of the parenting course. With the increase of single-parent homes, attention to the needs brought on by the absence of one parent should be part of an effective family ministry program. Yet care should be exercised in not calling too much attention to their single-parent status. After all, they are much more similar to dual parents than they are different. A delicate balance can be achieved.

What a tremendous opportunity for the church to affirm its single parents! The Lord can bring about good things in these homes as well as in dual-parent settings. A lot of single parents are doing an excellent job of raising their children in less than ideal circumstances. Let's focus on the positive and give our warm support and encouragement to the single-parent families among us.

• People-helping. The answer for a church concerned with the rise in fragmenting family and interpersonal relationships may not be to hire additional counselors. Even if more counselors were obtained, many people would resist their services. One of the most effective ways is to train mature lay people who have a gift for working with those who are troubled. This trend, which was started in the last decade among evangelicals, is an appropriate manifestation of the biblical doctrine of "one-anothering," a belief that advocates a shared responsibility for one another. Gary Collins and H. Norman Wright have written books and made tapes that are especially designed for that purpose.[9]

It is my experience and observation that about ten to twenty percent of an average congregation's membership will fall into the category of people-helpers who genuinely want to sharpen their interpersonal skills and have the ability and dedication to do so. Courses to train lay persons can either be worked into regular class times, or can be given at other times such as Sunday afternoons or weeknights. The participants can be selected by the church leaders, or the course can be open to anyone who desires to come. Certainly the leadership of the church should be involved in such training. Attention to this vital area of ministry will result in a multiplying of concerned helpers who are effective in dealing with people in personal or family crisis.

• Effective marriage and family communication. When asked to name the greatest problem they face in their families, most people will make reference to some form of communication difficulty. High interest and the relevance of the topic almost insure a successful session if the offering is planned well and publicized effectively. I recall one occasion when I offered a marriage communication course, limited to forty people. To my great surprise, over 140 preregistered for the course. A number of approaches can serve to generate and maintain interest. Small-group discussions, family chats, role playing, case discussions, and family group discussions are methods that produce experiential learning.

The format can include a midweek meeting of couples or entire families for a thirteen-week quarter within the regular church educational framework, or it can involve a series of weeknights outside the regular church meeting times, opening it up more to the community. Summer weeknights work best for some churches, when they can vary more from the normal routine and include appropriate films, panel discussions, etc., on topics of family communication. The weekend retreat setting, where families can get together and interact as a cluster, is an effective way to get some families who might be unable or unwilling to make a commitment to a regular meeting over a period of several weeks. Even though it is difficult to do so all the time, effort should be made to involve preschool children in at least some of the family activities. Carnes and Wright have some excellent material that can be adapted to family communication offerings.[10] Fairfield takes a biblical approach to marriage and family conflict, interweaving it with solid psychological principles to provide another good resource.[11]

• Family "together times." Many Christian families, with great initial resolve, have set out to have some sort of family devotional, perhaps on a daily basis at first, but the good intentions soon fell by the wayside. This oft-repeated frustration has caused some contemporary Christian authors to broaden their concept of the traditional family devotional, both in content and frequency. The time frame has been adjusted from daily to periodic (usually once a week is advocated). Content has expanded from prayer, Bible reading, and singing to a total approach emphasizing family relationships, informal settings, and applied Christianity. It emphasizes participation and permits spontaneity and flexibility, thus drawing the family unit closer together. Biblical themes and spiritual lessons are still taught, but within the context of informality. Evangelical magazines, such as Gospel Light's *Family Life Today*, offer outlined plans for weekly family nights. Wayne Rickerson has some excellent family night material, grouped according to children's ages.[12]

Two factors are integral to the success of a family night emphasis. One is that families and churches need to be committed to the concept, giving it high priority. Churches may have to schedule fewer committee meetings and other activities that regularly take family members out of the home. Family nights are not likely to occur on a widespread basis if there is not a collective awareness of and commitment to the concept.

The second key to the success of a family together time is the training of parents in how to plan and execute the activities. While this exercise may come naturally for a few families, the majority will not know how to begin, even though they may have a desire to do so. A workshop of about two hours may be enough to get the families started, if they are given creative ideas and resources for additional ideas. A church might even want to design its own family activities and distribute them through newsletters.

Another point that can be stressed in the instructional workshop is that the family times are for focused periods of togetherness and teaching but are by no means to be the *only* time of spiritual instruction. The effective religious and

moral development of children takes place all the time—
while riding in the car, eating a meal, walking, playing,
working—any time parents are together with their children.
This wholistic approach to teaching takes some of the pressure off the family together-time and relieves unnecessary
guilt if the event does not go as expected or does not take
place at all.

The point is that family nights are not going to happen on
their own by a simple announcement that they should. Commitment to the concept and training in the methods are
essential. And in that training, a proper perspective is desirable. From a personal standpoint, let me add that some of
the most meaningful times in our family have been in these
family night settings. I have learned more about my children—how they feel and what's going on inside them—
during these times of sharing than at any other time. Yet,
like many of you, we struggle periodically with the regularity and the content of these times. But the reward is well
worth the struggle.

• Family financial planning. Money matters are always
close to the top of the list when causes of conflict in American marriages are mentioned. The church's involvement
with this problem has traditionally been in the area of stewardship admonitions to bolster contributions, with an occasional sermon on the evils of materialism. The ten percent
or so that should be designated for the collection plate receives most of the attention. Ironically, Christian doctrine
states that *all* belongs to God, not just the ten percent. Con-
sequently, He is just as concerned about what happens to
the remaining ninety percent. Yet amazingly little attention
has been given to the wise stewardship of what is not "given
to God."

Churches have an excellent opportunity to develop short
courses on family financial planning.

The need is particularly great for instruction on budgeting, credit purchases, consumer fraud, wise investments, insurance needs, and estate planning. These courses could be developed by utilizing volunteers within the congregation who are professionally qualified. Workshops can also be offered to the community, using the same personnel.

• Building self-esteem in the family. Families in trouble have ceased affirming one another and have increased negative reinforcement. The strong presence of continual appreciation mutually expressed simply must be there. While many aspects of self-esteem could logically fall into the category of family communication or parenting, the topic is so important that it deserves special consideration.

James Dobson has done more than any other author to raise the level of awareness about the importance of self-esteem. His *Hide or Seek* received widespread acceptance. Since that publication, a number of authors have written about a proper Christian approach to self-esteem.

Since positive self-image is such an important key to children's successful adjustment in adulthood, it deserves its own place in courses and workshops on any aspect of family life. From a preventive standpoint, a myriad of future problems can be avoided when self-esteem is taught and applied in the family.

• Sex education. If the philosophy holds true that the educational burden falls primarily on the parents and not on the church, the sex education courses will be geared primarily toward parents, training them to educate their own children. Yet because all parents will not be involved in such an endeavor, the church may have to fill the void in a supplementary and secondary way. And weeknight or weekend workshops, with proper publicity, will attract community parents.

Sex education of the adults most often will have a better reception if it is incorporated into a marriage enrichment or marriage communication offering rather than promoted individually. It is difficult to offer workshops and seminars on human sexuality, even from a Christian standpoint, without running into social stigmas that sharply reduce attendance. Adults are more comfortable learning how to teach sexuality to their children than they are in learning about their own. The wise instructor will see that the two elements are skillfully blended.

At best, the whole area of sexuality is difficult to teach in any setting. Yet the necessity of saying something about the Christian and sexuality in a sincere and informed manner overshadows the difficulty in doing so. In contemporary times, it is mandatory that the Christian view of sexuality be presented as an alternative to the approaches devoid of a Christian perspective.

• Other offerings. Several other topics need to be mentioned as possibilities for the development of short courses, workshops, seminars, or part of larger offerings. Many have community appeal because they are problems common to all. Among the possible topics are:

—drug and alcohol abuse
—coping with death, terminal illness, and grief
—relating to aging parents
—mid-years crisis and the empty nest
—preretirement and retirement;
—topics dealing with singleness (widowed, divorced, never married)
—extended family and in-laws.

Perhaps some of these topics could be drawn together in a series, with a theme such as "Great Issues in Christian Living." Or take several of the education and prevention topics and highlight one per month for a year, with teaching and special activities focusing on each month's theme.

Do Something!
Two points in closing this chapter. First, this list of

suggested topics and areas for consideration is just a sampling of what could be done by a creative congregation. Let your mind take the basic ideas and come up with your own version. The big point is, do something! Most of these ideas don't cost a lot of money. If need be, they can be conducted in small groups in your home. Begin somewhere and do something to help strengthen families. The need is urgent and the task is great.

Footnotes

1. Psychological Publications, Inc., 5300 Hollywood Boulevard, Los Angeles, Calif. 90027.
2. David Olson, *Prepare: Premarital Personal and Relationship Evaluation.* Prepare-Enrich, Inc., P.O. Box 190, Minneapolis, Minn. 55440.
3. Family Life Publications, Inc., P.O. Box 427, Saluda, N.C. 28773.
4. *Ibid.*
5. Wes Roberts and Norman Wright, *Before You Say "I Do"* (Eugene, Ore.: Harvest House Publishers, 1978).
6. H. Norman Wright, *Premarital Counseling* (Chicago: Moody Press, 1977).
7. David R. Mace, *Close Companions: The Marriage Enrichment Handbook* (New York: Continuum, 1972), pp. 186-202.
8. *Ibid.*
9. Gary Collins, *How to be a People Helper* (Nashville: Vision House, 1976). H. Norman Wright, *Training Christians to Counsel* (Denver: Christian Marriage Enrichment, 1977).
10. P. J. Carnes, *Family Development I: Understanding Us* (Minneapolis: Interpersonal Communications Programs, Inc., 1981). Wright, *The Family That Listens* (Wheaton, Ill.: Victor Books, 1978).
11. James G.T. Fairfield, *When You Don't Agree: A Guide to Resolving Marriage and Family Conflicts* (Scottdale, Penn.: Herald Press, 1977).
12. Wayne Rickerson, see chapter 6 footnotes, note 3.

12
Specialized
Needs

C ertain groups within the fellowship of the church and beyond have special circumstances that require sustained attention. For several years churches have recognized the need for a ministry to young people. Almost every church has a youth program of some sort. Yet there are specific needs for other groups as well. We'll take a look at some of these specialized needs in terms of services to be offered. What follows is by no means comprehensive, but will be representative of ministries your church can offer. Let these suggestions serve as a catalyst for a lot more good ideas that would be especially suited to your own situation.

Growth Through Continuing Support
Mutual self-help groups, or support groups, are associations of individuals or family units that share the same problem, predicament, or situation and band together for the purpose of mutual aid. I prefer to call them *growth groups*, which adds a positive twist to their function. They have proved to be extremely beneficial in providing social support and promoting growth for the participants. This type of social

support serves to protect the people from the effect of certain stressors and promotes recovery from stress or crisis experienced as a result of life changes. These people need sustained support over a period of time in order to make the adjustment successfully. Churches are in an ideal position to develop support groups through a sensitive and caring program of family ministry.

The kinds of growth groups that can come out of this ministry are numerous. They are determined by the needs that are presented and usually focus around transition and crisis points in the family life cycle. A partial listing includes groups for widowed, divorced, stepfamilies, single parents, dual parents, children of divorced parents, bereaved parents, never-married singles, general sharing groups, handicapped people and/or their families, young marrieds, empty-nesters, marriage enrichment. Some churches are already involved in cooperating with groups such as Alcoholics Anonymous, Alanon, and Alateen, providing places for them.

Support groups need four basic ingredients in order to function at maximum effectiveness. They are in no particular order of priority and should be used together to produce the best results. First, the meeting should be a time of *information sharing*. People may come to these groups with insufficient or erroneous information about their particular situation. The sharing of correct information may help to clear up some of their confusion and point them toward a speedier solution. Advice-giving is not good information. The imparting of problem-solving techniques, where one assumes his or her own responsibility for the outcome, is good information.

A second element conducive to good support group meetings is *inspiration*. The emphasis is on creation of a positive atmosphere where the participants will have more hope and optimism when they leave than when they arrive. Some types of groups lend themselves better to a spiritual kind of inspiration than others do. In any event, it does not mean that negatives are not acknowledged and dealt with. It simply means that the overall tone of the meeting is a positive one.

The third element, *sharing interpersonal experiences*, is limited by the second in that the times of sharing and discussion are needed and desired, but should not be allowed to degenerate into seeing who has the worst experience in the group. The game called, "If you think that's bad, wait till you hear my story!" or "Now top this!" is fruitless and destructive. Focus can be directed by the leader to the present and future, with past "war stories" being minimized.

If the elements of a successful group experience were to be prioritized, perhaps the fourth, an *effective leader*, would head the list. The leader sets the tone for the group as he or she determines to a large degree the information, inspiration, and sharing of interpersonal experiences. The choice of who leads a particular group is a critical one because it often determines the success or failure of the group. Therefore, the following list may be helpful in the selection process:

• He or she should be trained to deal with people in a crisis situation, particularly in the area to which the support group ministers. Formal training is not a necessity; however, professionals who work in service-related fields such as social work, psychology, counseling, etc., should not be overlooked. Group leadership may give them an opportunity to volunteer their professional skills as Christians—a type of ministry often ignored by the church.

• The leader needs to be personally stable and mature, particularly if he has been through the crisis on which the present group is focused. A leader who is not emotionally recovered from a crisis may well compound the problem rather than contribute to the solution.

• Dependability and commitment to the task are essential to the life of the group. For that reason, it is generally a good

idea to have both a leader and a co-leader in order to provide consistency. A male and a female (not necessarily a
married couple) work well together in groups where both
sexes are involved.

• The leader is a facilitator more than a teacher and should
not provide quick answers to complex problems.

• The leader is a volunteer. No money need be spent to
hire group leaders. As a part of their ministry of outreach to
others, Christians can be persuaded to volunteer for this
important work. Some churches find that they are able to
exercise more positive control over the groups when the
leaders are chosen from their number. While this practice is
not always possible, guidelines for leaders should be set to
insure that the group meetings stay in keeping with the
overall philosophy of the church's family ministry program.

A few guidelines are appropriate for the meetings themselves.

—The meetings should be open to anyone in the community who has needs that a particular group is seeking to
meet. Mental health professionals and church staff people
in the area should be made aware of the group meetings.
This will help promote them to those who would benefit by
coming.

—It is helpful to have the meetings on a regular basis at
the same time each month. The frequency is usually once
a month, but some groups may need more. A check with the
group will reveal an acceptable schedule.

—It is best to have the meetings at the same location each
time. There is a running debate as to whether churches
should sponsor group meetings on-premises or off-prem-
ises. Each has its advantages and disadvantages. Churches
may have to use what facilities are available and most suitable. Consistency is perhaps more important than the particular location.

—The meetings should be fairly structured, with time

limits observed. A typical example might be information and inspiration from 7:30-8:00 P.M., discussion and sharing from 8:00-8:45 P.M., and refreshments from 8:45-9:00 P.M. Since some participants may have to arrange for baby-sitters, there needs to be a sensitivity to time demands.

—Since some people will feel ill at ease and self-conscious, particularly during the initial visit, they should not be forced to participate. The leaders should aim for a warm, informal, accepting environment.

One characteristic of a support group is that people will come and go as they see their own need. High turnover is the norm for some of these groups. This fact underlines the need for regularity of meeting times and dependability of the leaders, so that persons in distress can count on help being available at regular meeting times. The social support so desperately needed by hurting people is something they learn to appreciate through participation with others who share common concerns.

Programs for Older People

Because of the drastic problems facing youth and the climbing divorce rate among adults during the 1960s and 1970s, attention was focused away from older people in churches and in the society in general. Yet the dramatic changes occurring in the demographics of America necessitate a re-examination of this emphasis. By the year 2000, the median age will be 35 years, and one out of six Americans will be over 65.[1] As more people live longer, the church is faced with a monumental task of enhancing the quality and meaning of life through a ministry to older people. Fortunately, the neglect of earlier decades is now beginning to be corrected.

There are many myths and misconceptions about aging that plague society and the church. D.G. McTavish has captured them well, with his description of the typical view of older people as:

generally ill, tired, not sexually interested, mentally slower, forgetful, less able to learn new things, grouchy, withdrawn, feeling sorry for themselves, less likely to participate in activities (except, perhaps, religion), isolated, in the least happy time of life, unproductive, and loaded down with defense mechanisms and exaggerated neuroses.[2]

Most of these societal stereotypes are incorrect. The truth is that in both church and community older people are a great resource which has gone largely unnoticed and unused. Often their needs, brought on by significant life changes, also go unmet.

Churches would do well to seriously consider development of a program that would involve activities, instruction, fellowship, and ministry suitable to the needs and abilities of older adults. The program should reach beyond the borders of the church to include people in the community. A tremendous opportunity exists to minister to these people and to provide ways for them to serve other people. The finest talent, dedication, and wisdom the church has are to be found among older people, but their resources have scarcely been tapped. They have more time and, in some cases, more financial resource than other age groups in the church. The church can benefit greatly from organizing and mobilizing its older adults.

• Getting a program started. A step-by-step organizational procedure is offered only as a suggestion, with the hope that this will produce additional ideas. The first step is an important one—selection of one or two couples or individuals to be the coordinators of the program. The minimum age for them, as well as for the group they will lead, is 60 years. When the minimum age is lowered from 65 to 60 (or even 55), some people who are not yet retired can be a part of the program. By the time of their retirement, they will already be in the habit of participating. This approach is an attempt to counter the sometimes erroneous idea of those who say,

"I will wait until I retire; *then* I will get involved in the life of the church." (I always have a hard time finding those people when they retire!) The people who are chosen to head up the program need to be good motivators, organizers, and have proven leadership ability. It is also preferable that they not be deeply involved in other leadership responsibilities, so that they may be able to devote adequate time and attention to this important task.

In the early stages of the program, the coordinators should plan for a special emphasis weekend on older people, where the program will receive focused attention as it is launched. Perhaps a guest speaker who is familiar with the needs and potential of older adults may be invited to assist in the special emphasis. Ideally, the speaker will motivate and inspire the older adults in their new program and also inform the church as a whole about the possibilities of such a ministry. The leaders should also select a committee of five or six individuals or couples to be in charge of organizing various aspects of the ministry. Possible areas of involvement and appropriate committee assignments include: travel, fellowship, special events, visitation to shut-ins, community projects, special needs, telephone, arts and crafts, Bible study.

Perhaps the best way to launch the new program is with a fellowship dinner, during the special emphasis weekend, for all the church members who are 60 and older. At that event, the proposed programs can be explained. The people would then be given an opportunity to indicate their areas of interest and participation. Care should be given to assure prospective members—and leaders—that their commitment to involvement and responsibilities will be short-term and flexible. Since older people want to be away from home periodically, and since they prefer a more flexible schedule, an arrangement of frequent rotation of responsibilities seems to work best.

The initial meeting is also a good time for the participants to decide on a name for their group. They may decide on "The Thirty-Niners" or "Young at Heart" or "The Classics," or some creative name of their own choosing. Group identity and pride are important factors that need to be instilled from the beginning. One way of sustaining the continuity of the group is to have monthly fellowship meetings, where a meal and a light program are involved. Themes such as "Remember When," "Bring Your Wedding Pictures," "Western Night," and "Wear Something Old" are but a few of the many that are fun and create group cohesiveness. The meetings can also serve as effective communication points, where past activities and future plans are discussed. Monthly gatherings provide an excellent opportunity to invite guests from other churches and from the community.

• Program possibilities. Older adults know more than anyone else in what areas they should serve and be served. Therefore, the list of activities should come from them. Some activities already mentioned need further comment, as well as mention of a few additional ones.

The telephone committee, whose responsibility it is to construct a communication network among the older adults, can be involved in a vital ministry. The older people who live alone may need someone to check with them every day to inquire about their general well-being, as well as to provide some relationship. Responsibilities can be assigned through the committee to insure regular daily contact with these people.

Special information on Social Security, food stamps, Medicare, estate planning, insurance needs, home security, etc., can be made available to the group. One way would be to incorporate these presentations into a Community Bible Class, on a monthly basis. In the daytime or weeknight meeting, a short Bible study time could be followed by a presentation on relevant topics, such as the ones mentioned above. The meeting would provide yet another contact point of association with one another and with other older people in the community. Another service that could be offered to retired couples and individuals on fixed incomes is a free tax computation service each spring. Accountants and tax professionals in the church could be encouraged to donate a small portion of time each year for that purpose as their Christian ministry.

On occasion, a few of the older adults may be confined to their homes because of illness or injury. They may not need to be hospitalized but may still need periodic professional care. Christian nurses can perform a valuable service to these people by volunteering to check on them in their homes on a regular basis—in cooperation with their physicians, of course.

Many older men and women gladly volunteer to make home repairs for those who are unable to do so themselves. It instills in them a sense of worth and the satisfaction that comes from helping the helpless. Usually their know-how and ingenuity far exceed their younger counterparts, when it comes to repairs and remodeling.

One of the favorite activities of older adults is group travel. Some like one-day excursions, while others prefer long-distance trips. The group can decide where and when and how long. These together times will be special for those who participate.

Arts and crafts projects are perennial favorites. Quilting, ceramics, sewing, and the like provide quality time for interpersonal contact. A further aspect that can give these times additional meaning is the adopting of projects for hospitals, nursing homes, or orphanages and other charitable organizations. The sense of service and sharing adds importance to these activities.

A meaningful ministry of and for older adults can give them a renewed sense of value and contribution to others, while at the same time meeting their own social and spiritual concerns. For these reasons and more, a church ministry to older people is vitally important.

Programs for Young Parents

Development of programs for young parents goes beyond the mere provision of courses on raising young children. There is good rationale for emphasis on this particular phase of adulthood.

First, the transition into parenthood is a crisis point in the life cycle, both before and after the birth of the child. It is a mixture of positive and negative aspects and can be a time of concentrated marital stress, where the two, who have become one, now are three. Therefore, it deserves special attention.

Second, the early years of childhood are critically important in the psychological development of the child. Thorough education about this development will prevent future problems as the child grows into adulthood.

Third, young parents are likely to be more vulnerable to their own spiritual and moral condition, and to the future training of their child, than they will be at any other time in their lives. The church can have a meaningful ministry to them by providing instruction that will help them through this important time.

In light of the perceived needs of young parents, particularly mothers, the following programs could be offered to the community through the church's ministry to families:

• Prenatal courses that deal with more than the mechanics of giving birth and infant care can be offered. Emphasis should be placed on the husband-wife relationship, with encouragement to spend time together away from the baby. Changes in sexual feelings and desires should be addressed, as well as other emotional costs in parenting. As already mentioned, it would be a good time to talk about the moral and spiritual training of young children.

• A second course for new mothers, a sequel to the first, could be designed as a type of support group during the first year of the child's life. Meetings could be twice monthly, with an occasional night meeting to include husbands. Or the meetings could all be in the evenings, with husbands included. Some flexibility should be built into the curriculum to allow discussion of actual problems the participants are experiencing.

• New mothers in the community can be contacted by phone, mail, or personally by a volunteer, telling them of the services of the church's family ministry. Obviously, the size of the city is a determinant as to how thoroughly the job can be done. Cities of under 200,000 people are much easier to canvass than larger metropolitan areas. The church will also benefit from meeting young families who are unchurched or who have recently moved into the community.

• A "mother's day out" program is of real service to young mothers. It is a child-care program for preschool children at the church building one or two days a week. A small fee is usually charged to cover the cost of staffing and incidentals. It frees young mothers to run errands and have some time away from the constant pressure of child care.

The period of beginning parenthood is a complex one, complete with a mixture of joy and frustration. The "blessed event" can create a real strain on marriage. A family ministry program that is sensitive to these problems can offer an ounce of prevention and save a pound of trouble for the families involved.

Counseling Services
• The need. While the primary emphasis of the family ministry is on prevention of problems, rather than on therapeutic intervention, reality, nevertheless, demands that some provision be made to deal with marriage and family crises. If a church has an active outreach in the community, it will

invariably find families who are in real stress and need outside intervention. Also some people who take the preventive-oriented offerings of the church will see the need for individual attention to their problems. Churches that are involved in family ministries have an obligation to see that these counseling needs are met. They can offer the services themselves or see that they are provided through adequate referral services.

Who does the counseling? Of course, the members of the church staff carry their usual pastoral responsibilities. But the counseling I am talking about goes beyond pastoral advice. These counseling ministers have specialized training in the counseling process and in psychology. They are skilled in the techniques designed to bring about desired change. They may be volunteers in the church (social workers, school guidance counselors, etc.) or salaried full time or part time. We'll talk more about these considerations later.

• The emphasis. Since the program is family oriented, the emphasis in counseling should be on the family as a system.[3] This approach generally involves working with the entire family or in the case of marital dysfunction, working with both partners wherever possible. Especially for individuals with uncooperative spouses, group sessions may be preferred over individual sessions after an initial period of intake. Group sessions allow the counselor to spend his time more efficiently and allow the people to relate in a positive way to others who are experiencing similar difficulty. Small groups of couples and even families are also a possibility for groups.

Most church counseling services would do well to consider an emphasis on a short-term approach to therapy rather than an open-ended one. The visits should run on the average from six to eight visits per client(s). This approach accomplishes several things:

—It gives the counselor a time frame in which to work, a benefit for both counselor and client.

—It enables the counseling service to help more people by preventing long-term clients from dominating the counseling time.

—If people are aware of the time frame, they may be more willing to enter into the therapeutic contract and work harder at bringing about change within that time.

For those individuals or families who need more intensive and long-term assistance than the counseling service can offer, the counselor can perform a vital service by being an effective referral agent to put the people in touch with those who can help them. In order to perform this service, the counselor needs to be familiar with appropriate community resources. Since the counseling service cannot guarantee that every person's needs can be met, steps should be taken to identify the kinds of situations the service is equipped to assist. The gathering of background information, the initial interview, and the use of testing are helpful in making these assessments.

• Charges for counseling. Opinions vary among church people as to the advisability of charging fees for counseling in a church ministry. Those who favor a fee give these reasons:

—It is a meaningful part of the therapeutic process to require the client to invest something in the improvement of his or her life. One does not get "something for nothing," the reasoning goes.

—This method has shown that the client takes the therapy much more seriously and responds to the therapy quicker when he is financially involved.

—This approach eliminates time-consuming clients who are not really interested in improving themselves.

—The counseling service is above and beyond the normal services the church offers and, therefore, those who benefit from it should help pay for it (much like church-owned hospital services).

—The income derived from charging a modest fee for nonchurch members enables the center to offset expenses and broaden its ministry to help more people. (Most churches do not charge their own members for counseling services.)

—Most churches charge reduced fees (usually a sliding scale) in their counseling ministries, considerably less than community or private counseling fees.

—Counseling is more than a friendly chat sprinkled with pieces of advice. It is a form of therapy involving diagnosis and treatment of certain emotional and behavioral disorders that are hindering the person's social interaction and proper self-awareness. This function is much more than pastoral advice-giving and, therefore, the charge is legitimate to a client who receives these specialized services.

Those who oppose the charging of fees in a church counseling ministry point to the following:

—The church is to minister to people and should not sponsor any ministry that cannot be underwritten by the church.

—Some people who need help, but do not have the financial resources, will stay away.

—If there is a charge for counseling, the ministry of the church is not really distinguished from the nonchurch counselor who charges.

—The community and the church members may get some negative impressions of the church because of counseling fees.

Whichever method is chosen, a consensus opinion among the church leaders is the key to the decision. A number of churches are operating with success using each of the approaches. Still others set no fee for counseling services but rely on voluntary contributions from clients. *As a caution, these "contributions" are tax-deductible only if they do not go toward the financial support of the counselor but go directly to the church.*

Even among counseling ministries that do not charge for counseling time, it is customary for clients to be charged a "cost fee" for materials used, including tests, specially prepared forms, tapes, books, etc. Among those who charge fees, it is a general practice to: charge on a sliding scale according to ability to pay; never refuse anyone who needs help; and to give some special consideration to their own church members.

• Additional considerations. A program of this nature will obviously have a number of variables. The individual situation in each church and community will have to be taken into consideration in formulating a counseling ministry. In addition to the factors already mentioned, the following should be considered:

—What can be done and what cannot be done in a counseling ministry depends considerably on the kind and number of qualified personnel available. Skilled lay people can be used in some of the intermediate-level situations, but a person who has professional training in counseling needs to be involved as the director. Realizing capabilities and limitations is crucial to this kind of ministry.

—The relationship of church staff people to the counseling ministry, and their participation in it, will need to be clarified. If charges are made, this delineation is particularly important.

—People from the community will probably avail themselves of this service. It is likely that a counseling ministry will have a majority of its clients from other churches and from among the unchurched.

—The counseling program will be difficult to keep in perspective. If the overall thrust of your ministry is family enrichment and prevention of problems, it will be difficult to keep the proverbial "tail" of counseling from wagging the "dog"of family enrichment and prevention. If the director of the family ministry program is also doing some of the counseling, strict limitations of time spent in counseling may be needed to keep that arm of the ministry from dominating his or her time. Here is where the philosophy of family ministry touches practical decisions. Whether to spend the bulk of one's time devising ways for problems to be prevented, or to spend time with people for whom prevention is too late, is indeed a tough decision. The outcome depends on the philosophy of ministry, the stated goals, and the qualifications of the leaders.

Just a word of personal concern before going on to another topic. I hear a lot of church leaders say, "We don't want any counselor on our church staff. A family life educator, yes—but not a therapist." In one sense I agree with them. Yet I see the volume and intensity of personal and relational problems increasing, rather than going away. Somebody has to deal with these people. I would much rather a skilled Christian do it than a thoroughgoing secularist who has no regard for God. The issue is not whether we work with these troubled people, for surely we must. The real issue is whether we decide to meet the problem with staff who are trained and skilled or with staff who—though they have good hearts—don't know what they're doing. This is not a plea for professionalism; it *is* a plea for competence.

Resource Center

The resource center is a lending library of books, tapes, and periodicals on matters that relate to families. As a preventive tool it is invaluable in providing information to inquiring family members. This multipurpose library has the following uses:

• Books and tapes may be checked out by members of the sponsoring congregation on a two-week loan basis. If the resource center is open before and after some of the regular church gathering times, it will be used more than it would be otherwise.

• Materials can be checked out to community people with the director's approval. As a courtesy, the director may want to make the resources available to staff people of other churches and to community professionals.

• The library can be used by those who do counseling, both as a source of homework assignments for their clients and as a personal resource. All who work with people in a counseling or teaching role need the latest and the best resources available to aid them in their ministry. Since most of the material has a Christian perspective, it would not likely be found in a public or university library. A good resource center is also essential if the family ministry program is going to produce some of its own curriculum.

• The library can be used as an aid in training programs for church leaders and skilled Christian helpers. The periodicals in particular provide a good source of information in compact form for the ongoing education of people who work with families.

• Something that should be seriously considered is a children's section. Books on the preschool and elementary age levels can be selected around the general theme of family relationships, growth in interpersonal relationships, religious and moral teaching, self-image, etc. Because of the interest in reading that most children have, this special section for them may be one of the most frequently used portions of the resource center. An added benefit occurs when the parents, who bring the children to the library, are likely to browse among the other books and select one or two for themselves.

Funding for the resource center can be accomplished in a number of ways. It can be a regular budgeted item from the beginning or it can be added to the budget at a later time. The best way to begin the library is through a special contribution that will insure the quick collection of a sizable amount of materials. This method will also serve to call attention to the new resources available.

One good way to keep the library stocked with a steady stream of new materials is to have a month-long book drive each year during a time when there is not a lot of other activity going on (perhaps late winter or early spring). The book titles or books themselves can be placed in the church foyer or Sunday School classrooms, where people can make their donation selections and pay for the books. They can also be encouraged to donate as memorial gifts, honoring deceased relatives and friends in a lasting and useful way.

Church libraries are notorious for their lack of use. Yet the family-life resource center can grow to become the hub of the family ministry program. Vital to the reaching of that goal is effective promotion of the library and development of a good volunteer force trained to manage all aspects of the library.

Footnotes

1. "The Graying of America," *Newsweek*, February 28, 1977, pp. 50ff.
2. D.G. McTavish, "Perceptions of Old People: A Review of Research Methodologies and Findings," *Gerontologist*, 1971, *11*, pp. 90-101.
3. For an excellent introduction to working with families as a system in the church setting, see J.C. Wynn, *Family Therapy in Pastoral Ministry* (New York: Harper & Row, 1982).

13
Getting It
All Started

A program is virtually useless as long as it exists only on paper. The actual method of implementation of the various ministries is a critical one, often making the difference between success and failure of the overall program. Therefore, let's look at a series of questions that must be dealt with in order for the family life outreach to become a reality. Failure to deal with these issues will result in poor execution of what might otherwise be an excellent program. After the questions, we will consider some matters that need attention once the decision has been made to develop a family ministry.

Questions to Ask in Considering a Family Ministry

• *Does the congregation see a need for improved family life?* There is a vast difference in potential between a few vocal members in favor of a family emphasis and a widespread interest and support of such a program. An accurate assessment needs to be made as to the need for this ministry as seen by the average church member. Where there is no perceived need, there is no support.

The first step may be an awareness campaign to highlight local and church family needs and the potential a family ministry can offer. The minister can preach several sermons that will help raise the awareness level. Usually a trip to the county courthouse to examine family-related statistics results in plenty of local evidence for a need to minister to families. Asking for a show of hands from those in your congregation whose families have been affected in some way by divorce is another graphic way of showing how the current family breakup is affecting Christians.

An integral part of the awareness campaign should be the introduction of some of the foundations of family ministry previously discussed. Particularly helpful is the theological justification and the rationale for prevention of problems as the most effective way of countering the present trend. As much as six months' lead time may be needed to prepare the congregation for a proper response to the presented needs.

• *Is the congregation prepared to do something about it?* Being aware of the need for a family ministry program is not enough. Determination should be made as to whether the church is prepared to take steps to implement such a program. One helpful tool, both in assessing the needs of families and in determining interest, is the development of a questionnaire that can be administered to the congregation. Some type of polling of the congregation's degree of need and willingness for action will have its benefits.

• *What is the commitment of various leaders toward improving the quality of family life in the church and the community?* Three levels of leadership need particular attention. Variations of these levels will depend on the church's organizational structure. Perhaps the most central figure in determining whether a family ministry emphasis will be a success or failure is the pulpit minister. He is the major opinion-setter in the congregation and its public proclaimer. Family emphases are difficult to begin without the public support of the person who stands before the people every Sunday and who is also a key representative of the church to the community. His public endorsements are invaluable publicity, and his silence on these matters (not to mention his opposition) can be damaging.

Another level of leadership whose commitment needs to be assessed is the body of local lay leaders, variously known as elders, board, or deacons. Their degree of support for the program among the people at large is another key factor in determining its success. One way of getting their support and involvement is to draw heavily from their number in formulating a feasibility committee, whose task it will be to assess the congregational needs and the possibility of developing a family ministry program.

The third level of leadership whose involvement is necessary in the early stages is the entire church staff. They need to understand the integrative nature of the family ministry approach and be able to see how their individual areas of emphasis can benefit from such an approach.

• *Who is the ministry designed to reach?* A decision needs to be made among three alternatives. First, the program may be designed primarily to meet the family needs of members of the local congregation. Many family ministry programs have as their target group their own people. While outsiders may on occasion be involved, the thrust is largely an intracongregational one—the enrichment of church families.

A second option is to focus not on the congregation but primarily on the people in the community. Few programs of this nature exist, although in the social gospel movement of the late nineteenth century, an emphasis in that direction prevailed among certain churches.

The third approach, and the most desirable one, is a blending of the first two. The combination of church family enrichment and community family enrichment is an ideal one, since the church is to be an influencing agent for good in its

surrounding society. A community outreach emphasis con-
vinces people that the church is serious about being of service to them by meeting their deeper needs. Also, unchurched people will tend to be more responsive to the
spiritual dimension of their lives when they see assistance
given them by the church in a time of stress or crisis. A
proper tension in the emphases on church and community
families is not easy to maintain, but the rewards in achieving this are worth the effort. It says to a community that the
church is interested in what happens to their families.

• *What does the leadership and membership think ought to
be done to deal with family problems?* For some churches,
especially the larger ones, involvement in family ministry
might mean the hiring of additional personnel, either on a
full-time or a part-time basis. While paid staff positions are
not a necessity in starting the program, the size and scope
of the ministry might demand staff additions. If a person is
hired, care needs to be given to his qualifications and
strengths. For instance, a person skilled in counseling techniques may have little ability or interest in administrative
and promotional work, and vice versa. Probably the most
important quality a director of a family life ministry can
have is promotional and administrative skill combined with
the technicalities of family interaction. Since volunteer
management is integral to the work, this should also be
considered.

• *Will there be a need for additional space? Or can present
buildings be used with some adjustment?* Flexibility is the
watchword here. Churches who have need for additional
facilities, and resources to build them, will want to proceed.
But lack of ideal facilities should not be a deterrent to some
kind of beginning. Existing structures can be used until better ones come along. For the community courses, off-prem-
ises locations such as public schools or meeting halls can
perhaps be used. Some church counselors believe that a

building separate from the sanctuary is helpful for counseling, particularly as it involves community people. Counseling confidentiality of the clients needs to be respected.

• *What type of family ministry is anticipated?* Several factors enter into the answer to this question. What is developed will depend on talent and resources available. The church's philosophy also figures into the direction of the ministry. Not all programs have to be developed at once. They can be introduced gradually, as the ministry grows and as the needs become evident. Care should be taken to begin with offerings that have a high predictability rate for success. Your church surveys should give you some clues as to areas of high need and interest.

• *What kind of personnel does the church have or anticipate?* In addition to the staffing needs that have already been considered, the formulators of a family emphasis will want to look in two other directions. The first is toward the existing staff and any possible contributions they could make to the overall programs. One person may be able to assist in counseling a few hours a week, while another may be willing to teach a parenting course, while still another can help with family retreats. The spirit of cooperation and involvement at the staff level prevents the family ministry from taking on the appearance of an isolated, self-contained program that has little to do with other areas of staff responsibility.

Apart from the paid staff, volunteers with professional skills and general volunteers are essential to the ongoing programs of a family ministry outreach. The church cannot and should not pay for all the work involved. Christians have an excellent opportunity to be involved as volunteers on various levels for counseling, yard work, library maintenance, secretarial work, and the many other ministries connected to this program. A family ministry committee, composed of lay couples or individuals in the church, may be the best way to plan and coordinate all the activities.

• *What services of a similar nature are available through community organizations and other churches?* Planners need to be aware of the types of offerings that are available elsewhere. In some cases, duplication is needless and should be avoided. For example, except in large metropolitan areas, there may be no real need for a support group for bereaved parents if a local chapter of Compassionate Friends (a national organization of bereaved parents) is already active. Other services, because of the widespread need for them, could legitimately be duplicated, such as divorce support groups, widows' groups, parenting and marriage enrichment courses, etc. Encourage a spirit of cooperation with activities of a similar nature.

• *What kind of media exposure and publicity can the church expect, to make known its ministry?* Promotion to the public is the lifeblood of an effective family outreach. A church may have one of the finest programs available anywhere; but if the community does not know about it, the program cannot strengthen its families. The degree of media influence varies from city to city. For example, in one city the newspaper is especially strong as an opinion-setter and is widely read. In another city, it may be a particular television station. Rating reports and conversations with established community leaders will reveal where the influence is. In advertising upcoming programs, one fifteen-second television spot well placed may reach many more people than a morning and evening newspaper advertisement. Television newspeople and newspaper staff (especially religion editors) can give the ministry a lot of free publicity by reporting on events of community interest. The director should take care to develop relationships with these media people.

In addition to newspaper and television coverage, several other effective kinds of promotion should be noted:

—Radio spots are helpful in promoting upcoming events. For radio use, be aware of the population covered and the target age group of the station. As in television and newspaper promotion, the lowest rate may not be the best buy.

—Brochures telling about the program and a schedule of its offerings are effective, provided they are professional in appearance. Develop a mailing list that includes local mental health professionals, social agencies, school personnel, clergymen, physicians, attorneys, judges, city officials—people who deal with troubled families.

—Representatives from the family outreach program can make themselves available for speaking engagements at local school PTA meetings, civic luncheons, hospital programs, etc., telling their audiences about the services available to anyone in the community.

—Some of the most effective and efficient advertising can be done by the church people who help sponsor the ministry and by satisfied participants who have personally benefited from the ministry.

• *What size area will this ministry cover?* Size of the city is a determining factor. The approach of a small town church will be significantly different than that of an urban church. The size of the area to be covered will also play a major role in the type and method of advertising. Other factors to be considered include:

—the pressing needs of the town or area
—type of people living within the area of influence (sociological factors such as race, economics, social status)
—location of the church facilities.

All these elements blend with the overall approach of the ministry to produce a unique program with maximum potential for a particular set of circumstances.

• *Who is the church trying to reach in that area?* Related to the former question is this present one that requires identification of target groups of people. To simply "aim for everyone" may well be like a shotgun blast that hits nothing. Each church has particular interests and strengths and appeals to certain groups of people, and these are going to manifest themselves in a family emphasis. While everyone should be welcomed, the effort will generally draw certain types of people more than it will others.

This issue becomes a complex one, particularly for a homogeneous church. While a particular program may have a primary target group, troubled families, and those who want to enhance the quality of their life together, will come from diverse backgrounds. No attempt here is being made to settle the issue of who to anticipate and what to do with those who come. My purpose here is to present the problem and suggest that it has to be dealt with in a spirit of flexibility and adaptability.

• *What is the role of evangelism in a family ministry?* Evangelism is a legitimate enterprise for a church in a family ministry. From a Christian perspective, the spiritual dimensions of family problems cannot be ignored. But *how* evangelism enters in is crucial. If community people discover that the family programs are offered as a thinly veiled front for high-pressure evangelism of a sectarian variety, the public aspect of the program is doomed. In counseling situations, when a desperate person comes for help with a crisis situation and is given only spiritual commands to be saved by doing "this or that," or told that all his problems are because of sin in his own life, great damage can occur.

It is unethical for a counselor to take advantage of a person in a state of crisis, whose confusion level is high, and who is desperate enough to do anything that an authority figure tells him to do. A much better approach is for the counselor to first help the person deal with the immediacy of the crisis. Then after things are beginning to be resolved, *with the person's consent* the counselor may wish to deal with the spiritual implications of his or her circumstances and discuss what action would be appropriate. The religious dimension is legitimate and desirable, but in its rightful context.

• *Are there ways that congregations could combine their resources on a city-wide basis to build a family life ministry?* In certain situations a church might be unable to offer a particular program alone but could do so on a cooperative basis with others. Most aspects of family ministry to the public lend themselves to cooperative efforts either within denominational frameworks or on an interdenominational basis.

—Several community Christian counseling services are in existence, where a number of churches help underwrite the cost for establishing and maintaining a counseling clinic staffed with counselors who are Christians.

—Special series of films and speakers can be co-sponsored in a joint community effort.

—Course offerings, marriage enrichment weekends, family retreats, workshops, and seminars can be jointly sponsored at several levels.

Cooperative efforts are generally more cost-effective than individual ones. Churches may do well to investigate their common goals of enriching family life and work together toward seeing them realized. By so doing, they will have more impact on community family life than any one of them could alone.

How to Begin
The assumption in this section is that a decision has been made by a church to begin a family life program. The material that follows is a checklist of matters that need attention. The Family Ministry Committee can oversee development of the program. Committee members should be chosen from a variety of family situations and age categories. If members have particular talents and interests, the chairperson is able to assign responsibilities in those areas.

• *Assessment study.* The first order of business, if it has not already been done, is for the committee to bring together the various questions raised in the previous section and provide some coherence and direction to the answers. The goals for the program should come from the foundations of family ministry. Therefore, attention to the basic philosophy is a beginning point. After arriving at the methods of accomplishing the stated goals, the committee will then be able to deal with matters like location, director, role of counseling, financing, and integrative aspects of the program. In most cases, the committee is in a much better position to formulate these goals and methods of accomplishment than a newly hired director of the program, because they know the church and the community.

The bulk of this groundwork needs to be done by the church members before additional personnel are considered. The exception is where a present staff member would be assuming the directorship. In that case, he or she could be involved in the planning from the beginning. A new person being considered would need to know some general directions and philosophical assumptions before a decision could be made as to his or her compatibility with the program.

• *Finances.* Several matters need to be discussed in determining the financial operations of the family ministry program.

—How much will be budgeted annually? For churches with larger programs, the added expenses—particularly where personnel are involved—may alter the church budget upward considerably.

—Will there be a need for a special contribution to get the program started? An excellent way of creating interest and awareness of the new ministry is to designate a particular Sunday as "Family Ministry Sunday" and give the congregation an opportunity to help establish the program on a solid financial footing. The special contribution can be an effective way of providing initial funds that would not otherwise be available.

—What is to be done with contributions to the ministry once it has been started? The decision on counseling fees or contributions becomes a key factor here. In addition to that source of income, individuals in the church, and those in the community who have been helped, may on occasion give money to the ministry. Some guidelines need to be set ahead of time with those who are charged with church financial matters about what to do with these unrestricted gifts.

—How will the financial records of the ministry be kept? It is helpful, wherever possible, to keep a separate set of books on the ministry. These records will tend to be more complex than those of other ministries, primarily because a family ministry has the potential to be income-producing.

• *Evaluation.* It is important from the beginning stages of the proposed new ministry to define ways of evaluating its success. Some of the family enrichment goals are qualitative in nature and are therefore difficult to measure. A long-range evaluation (three to five years) is more realistic in determining increase in the quality of family life in the church. Nevertheless, various methods of short-range evaluation should also be used:

—Evaluation sheets can be given for participants to complete at the end of each educational offering.

—Follow-up can be done on premarital class participants to determine the effectiveness of instruction.

—The degree of involvement on the part of church members, both as volunteers and participants, is a good indicator of the degree of success.

—General community attitudes toward the program and the degree of response to the offerings will show whether the stated purposes are being fulfilled.

—The verbal feedback from church members about the effectiveness of the program is another good indicator.

—Records of educational offerings and counseling clients will give information that indicates the type of impact the ministry is having.

158 / Building Stronger Families

Evaluation should be a continual practice and a welcomed one. An annual report, supplemented with a six-month report, is helpful in taking stock of the program's progress. Copies of the reports should be distributed to the leaders of the church in an effort to keep them informed; annual reports should be made to the church at large. A strong sense of flexibility and willingness to change is essential for the success of a new program. There is no way to anticipate how well certain efforts within the program will meet the needs of the families involved. Thus the need for continual pulse-taking on the progress toward the goals, and for wisdom and courage to make changes when they are called for.

• *Presentation of program.* The timing and manner of presenting the new family ministry program to the church and to the community is important. Lead time of several weeks is preferable, especially if the official beginning is marked with a special contribution. Advance announcements also provide a possibility for free media coverage. The day for the initial announcement should be chosen carefully, with a minimal overlap with other events. In the church, the beginning of the ministry can set the tone for the future; therefore, the time and effort put into the planning of its inauguration is well invested.

14
Working Together for Heaven's Sake!

F amily-life ministry of the church as I have described it has much to do with the *nature* of the church. The church of the New Testament is more like a family than anything else. The body life of a church fellowship at its finest should parallel good family interactions. While we might all agree with these assertions, some contemporary, institutionally oriented churches find the implications of these simple statements staggering. Fundamental changes are necessary to switch from a task-oriented business model to a relationship-oriented family model.

I admire the work of Charles Sell, Director of the School of Christian Education at Trinity Evangelical Divinity School. He has established himself as a leader in the field of family ministry. His work on *Family Ministry*, published in 1981, made him one of the chief architects of a family ministry theology, along with Larry Richards and Gene Getz. I use his book in my graduate class on Family Ministry. He has a lot of good things to say about the nature of the church and the kind of ministry it should have toward families. In a section entitled "The Family-Church Family,"[1] he lists twelve principles that arise out of a convergence of theological guidelines, educational insights, and needs of families. While the practical outcome in individual churches will certainly vary, I believe these principles are central for our consideration. They blend beautifully the partnership of family and church that is essential for a meaningful, biblical ministry. To summarize the material in this second part, I present them for your consideration.

1. *Family life concepts are best communicated by the church's total expression of family relationships and values.*

They must be integrally related into the life of the church rather than an appendage tacked on. The nature and function of the church are familylike. Organization is not negated in the process, but it certainly is redefined. The family analogy permeates the New Testament concept of the church. In fact, it is more than an analogy—it is a dynamic experience that links family life and church life inextricably together.

2. *Family-life education can be built into existing programs and can be an ongoing ministry.*

From the standpoint of time demands on the family, it makes sense to integrate a family emphasis as much as possible into already established meeting times. From a financial and personnel standpoint, it is expeditious.

3. *Family life should not be hindered by the life of the church, since home and church, both of God's design, should not be competitive.*

We hope that in the future the joy of the home-church partnership will increasingly replace the frustration of competition. As the church-as-a-family concept grows, so will the joy.

4. Christian education should be carried out in both the home and the church with an integral program and plan.

The collective body can provide our families with Christian experiences that would be difficult, if not impossible, to achieve with individual efforts. But the church will always remain a *supplement* to family nurture, and not a *substitute* for it.

5. Provision should be made for children who have no Christian parents, but evangelistic programs for children should be accompanied by an adequate evangelistic ministry aimed at their parents.

Children who are in our churches without their parents are certainly important and need our special attention. But their chances of staying faithful to Christ are greatly enhanced when their parents are also involved. Outreach to entire families is better than just to the children.

6. Family-life emphasis should include family forms other than nuclear, with every effort being made to protect them from being left out.

A family ministry too narrowly defined may cause more heartache than help. All legitimate family makeups, including singles, need to feel a part of the church family. Sensitivity and balance in a program will meet the needs of all family forms.

7. Intergenerational experiences can be intentionally designed, but the total church program should provide for regular informal interaction between generations.

What a beautiful sight to see all those grandmas and grandpas and grandkids and brothers and sisters loving one another! And learning from one another. And being encouraged by one another. The church family needs more integration of the age groups, not more segregation.

8. Laymen should be enlisted for various phases of family-life ministry.

Widespread involvement of church members is a critical key to this emphasis. They can be trained and can then teach others, which is what Paul encouraged Timothy to do (2 Tim. 2:2). The church needs more people-helpers!

9. New family programs might be initiated on a voluntary basis.

For a number of reasons, it is best not to force or pressure people into family-life offerings. Some may not be interested, others may feel threatened by it, and still others may have other greater needs. Always emphasize the voluntary nature of participation, perhaps offering alternatives to those with other interests. Then go with the people you have, and do not intimidate those you don't have.

10. Attempts to influence the family should give priority to the training of fathers for their role.

The Bible and many modern family specialists agree that the father is the primary change agent in the home life. He is also the primary transmitter of values and morals. Obviously, the mother's influence is tremendously significant, as well. We need a balanced approach, also including some "catch-up" work in training Christian fathers.

11. The church life and program should communicate and be built on the concept that the parents are responsible for the child's nurture (Deut. 6; Eph. 6:4).

That primary task of parents cannot be handed to anybody else. Home and church need unity, not dichotomy. Yet, in their joining, the essential responsibility of parents as the primary source of spiritual development for their children cannot be abdicated.

12. The teaching and training ministry of the whole church body should be related to family life.

Notice the ease with which New Testament writers of the Epistles blend theology with home life and family relationships. So it should be today. The family should be the laboratory of Christian living; therefore illustrations of belief and practice in the church should take family-life situations into consideration.[2]

Will family ministry work in the church? I believe with all my heart it will. These ideas I have put before you are workable for three reasons:

• Family ministry is biblical.
• It meets a great need.
• It builds up and edifies.

In one way or another, I have tried to weave these convictions throughout everything I have said. The proof of the effectiveness of these efforts lies in the positive difference it makes for you. My prayer for you is that you will believe you can make a difference in your own family and in your church and community. With God's help, we *can* build stronger families!

Footnotes

1. Charles M. Sell, *Family Ministry: Family Life Through the Church* (Grand Rapids: Zondervan), pp. 74-94.
2. Adapted from Charles M. Sell, *Family Ministry*, pp. 91-93.

Acknowledgments

I suppose the writer of Ecclesiastes was right: there is nothing new under the sun. In the world of my own ideas that is certainly the case. It seems that every time I come anywhere near approximating what might be some "new" idea, I soon read about someone else who has refined it and done a much better job than I in making it sensible and useful.

Many of my ideas about families, and particularly about family ministry, were shaped out of my own experiences in ministry to families. And yet it is refreshing to come across people who share those same ideas and have done a good job in articulating them. Such is the case with three people in particular in regard to the present work. The influence of Dr. Nick Stinnett will be obvious to you. The discovery of Dr. Charles Sell through his book, *Family Ministry*, was a delightful one for me. Here was a man who was saying many of the same things I had found to be true. And he said them so well! Also, I came across the work of Dolores Curran in her *Traits of a Healthy Family*, just when I was finishing this book. She was a blessing to me also because she confirmed once again some convictions about families that I have held for a long time.

Many people contribute to who we are and what we believe. I owe a special debt of gratitude to my own marvelous family, who continually provide me unforgettable experiences of what it means to be a strong, loving family. And to God, who continually showers me with His inexpressible gifts, I give my deepest thanks.

Royce Money
Abilene, Texas
1984